P9-DNZ-132

Take a Hike!

Take a Hike!

The Sierra Club Kid's Guide
to Hiking and Backpacking

LYNNE FOSTER
Illustrated by Martha Weston

Sierra Club Books | **Little, Brown and Company**
San Francisco | Boston • Toronto • London

The Sierra Club, founded in 1892 by John Muir, has devoted itself to the study and protection of the earth's scenic and ecological resources — mountains, wetlands, woodlands, wild shores and rivers, deserts and plains. The publishing program of the Sierra Club offers books to the public as a nonprofit educational service in the hope that they may enlarge the public's understanding of the Club's basic concerns. The Sierra Club has some sixty chapters in the United States and in Canada. For information about how you may participate in its programs to preserve wilderness and the quality of life, please address inquiries to Sierra Club, 730 Polk Street, San Francisco, CA 94109.

Text copyright ©1991 by Lynne Foster
Illustrations copyright ©1991 by Martha Weston

All rights reserved. No part of this book may be reproduced in any form or by any electronic or mechanical means, including information storage and retrieval systems, without permission in writing from the publisher, except by a reviewer who may quote brief passages in a review.

First edition

Library of Congress Cataloging-in-Publication Data

Foster, Lynne, 1937–
    Take a hike! : the Sierra Club kid's guide to hiking and backpacking /
Lynne Foster ; illustrated by Martha Weston. — 1st ed.
        p.   cm.
    Includes bibliographical references and index.
    Summary: Explains how to prepare for and enjoy hiking and backpacking.
    ISBN 0-316-28948-5
    1. Hiking — Juvenile literature. 2. Backpacking — Juvenile literature.
[1. Hiking. 2. Backpacking.] I. Weston, Martha, ill. II. Title.
GV199.5.F65 1990   90-8803
796.5'1 — dc20

10 9 8 7 6 5 4 3 2 1
BP

Sierra Club Books / Little, Brown children's books are published by Little, Brown and Company (Inc.) in association with Sierra Club Books.

Published simultaneously in Canada by
Little, Brown & Company (Canada) Limited

Printed in the United States of America

*This book is for John Dorian,
one of my favorite up-and-coming hikers*

Contents

1
Getting Started

If you actually ask people why they go hiking or back-packing and how they got started doing it, they may have a hard time answering you. After thinking about the question for a minute, some people might say they go because they love the mountains (or the desert, or the seashore, or some other kind of place). Others might say they want to "get away from it all." Many will certainly say they go because it's so much fun. Most will say their friends or family talked them into trying hiking and backpacking.

But why don't these folks get away from it all by pic-nicking at the nearest park? Or "visit" the mountains by reading a travel book? What's fun about slogging up a trail, maybe meeting bears and snakes, running into poison ivy and mosquitoes, maybe getting lost, getting rained on, eating weird food, sleeping on rocks, and not having any bathroom? What did their friends and family say to them that made them want to leave all the comforts of home, put on a pack, and work up a sweat on some trail into the wilds?

If you're patient and talk to enough hikers and backpackers, after a while you'll discover that hikers don't usually slog up trails. They walk up them slowly, while talking with their friends and enjoying the scenery, the fresh air, the flowers, and the wildlife. You'll find out that bears and snakes hardly ever get close enough for hikers to see them — and that these animals are too busy living

their own lives to be much interested in you. You'll hear that it's easy to avoid poison ivy and to fend off mosquitoes. You'll learn that walking in the rain with the right gear can be an adventure.

As for weird food, hikers will tell you that on the trail you can eat just about the same way you do at home, if you want to (and that you get to snack a lot). They may also mention the great views to be had from most outdoor "bush stops." And they'll certainly clue you in to the fact that when you're looking up at the stars from a cozy sleeping bag atop a comfortable foam pad, even rocks aren't a problem.

In fact, by the time you finish your hiker and backpacker survey, you'll probably be ready to rush off to the nearest trail, so you can get in on the good times. But before you do, there are some things you need to know, such as exactly where you're going and how to get there — and back. You also need to find out what kinds of food and clothes and gear you'll need and what to do if something goes wrong. Then there are camping-out skills. And you'll probably want to have some idea of what you might see along the trail.

All these things are the basics of hiking and backpacking, which is what this book is about. Soon you'll be ready to start off down (or up) those trails and find out for yourself what a great adventure it is to hike and backpack. So let's get started!

Hiking Is for Everyone

Even if we're not hikers yet, most of us spend quite a bit of time walking. We may walk to school, to a friend's house, to the store, to the refrigerator, to our classes, to where we keep our bike, and so on. Hiking, then, is just more walking in different places, right?

The answer is "Yes and no." Yes, hiking is walking. No, it's not *just* walking. You might say, for instance, that when you take a walk, you really don't need any equipment. Of course, if you're walking to the store, you'll probably take along some money. If you're walking to the library, you may be carrying some books. But because you're close to home — and to food, water, and clothes — you don't need to bring along much of anything else.

When you take a hike, most of the time you won't be close to the comforts of home. You're more likely to be in a park or a forest, at the beach or in the mountains, maybe in the desert or in an unfamiliar part of your own town. And when you're not close to the comforts of home, you need to take some of them with you, even if you're hiking on a sidewalk or a road instead of a trail.

That's why nearly all hikers you see are carrying some sort of pack. Hikers who are out for a few hours or even a whole day think of themselves as *day hikers*. They usually carry a few comforts with them in a *day pack*. If you looked into the average hiker's day pack, you might find

ON A WALK | DAY HIKING | BACKPACKING

a jacket, a lunch and snacks, some sunscreen, water, a map, a small flashlight, a basic first aid kit, and a litter bag.

Hikers who are planning to stay out overnight need a larger pack — a *backpack* — because they need to take along more comforts than hikers who are only going to be away for a few hours or for a day. If you looked inside a backpacker's pack, you might find a small tent, food for several meals, a cup and spoon, perhaps a tiny back-packer's stove and some fuel, a cooking pot, extra clothes, and a warm jacket, as well as the usual day hiker supplies. A sleeping bag, ground cover, and pad (in waterproof stuff sacks) would probably be attached to the outside of the pack with straps.

Of course, more equipment means more planning, and more planning usually requires more experience. That's why most folks start out with day hiking instead of with backpacking. Just about anyone can become an "instant" day hiker. You don't even need a trail — a sidewalk or a road will do if there aren't any trails nearby. (In fact,

sidewalks are one of the best places to start your hiking career. You could even take your first day hike to a store that sells day packs!)

Not everyone who takes day hikes goes on to back-packing. There are all kinds of hikers. Some people like nice, flat trails with lots of flowers and birds. Some like steep trails with spectacular views. Some like trails with a mountain peak at the end (these hikers are sometimes called "peak baggers"). Some like short trails, some like long trails. Some like faraway trails, some like trails close to home. Some like day hikes, some like backpacking trips, and some like both. But they all like hiking!

Getting in Shape

As you can see, there are about as many different kinds of hikes as there are people who take them — from short, easy hikes for people who haven't done much walking lately to long, tough hikes for people who are in shape and like to exercise hard. There are also plenty of hikes in between for people who are on their way to being in shape.

When some people start hiking, they already have strong leg muscles and can walk up a hill fast without feeling as if their legs and breath are going to give out before they get to the top. These people probably walk quite a bit every day. Instead of going to school by car, they may ride a bike. Instead of taking a bus to the movies, they may walk.

Many people who want to start hiking haven't done much walking and aren't in very good shape, but they can start hiking and still enjoy it as much as the people who are in better shape. They just need to start out with shorter, easier hikes. After a few hikes, they'll be in better shape and will be able to take longer, harder hikes if they want to.

Hikers who go backpacking are usually in good shape — they have to be in order to carry the comforts they need for staying out on the trail overnight. But people aren't born in good shape — they have to *get* in good shape.

Luckily, getting in shape for hiking and backpacking isn't hard at all. The main thing you need to do is walk more and walk harder. If the thought of walking more doesn't thrill you, think of each walk as a hike. Start out by hiking to a friend's house. Hike to the store. Hike to the movies. Hike to the roller rink. Hike to school. Hike to the park for a day hike. Take along a friend whenever you can!

Of course, lots of other kinds of exercise besides walking will help you get in shape — bicycling, for instance, and roller skating. Swimming, surfing, playing tennis, jogging, and dancing are all good ways to get in shape, too. And remember that you should be getting your whole body in shape, not just your legs. You need strong arms and shoulders so you can take a loaded pack off and put it on easily. Try to walk somewhere every day. But also try some other kinds of exercise several times a week. Before you know it, you'll be in shape for the trail.

Trail Gear

The gear that hikers put in their packs can be sorted into three groups: "must take," "very useful," and "for fun." Food is an example of the first ("must") kind. A bandanna is in the second ("useful") group. And binoculars fall into the third ("fun") category. Keep in mind that no matter what group a piece of trail gear is in, it should be lightweight. Now let's start by talking about day-hiking gear.

A Day-Hiking Start-up List

Although you don't need much gear for day hiking, it's almost all important. As you'll see, most of it falls into the "must take" group.

Small day pack (a must). "Small" is the word to remember here. When you buy your first day pack, it's easy to go "big." Resist the temptation. Enjoy looking at all those roomy, fancy day packs, but don't buy one. Day packs are sort of like closets. If the space is there, it gets filled up. And if you don't fill it, someday your friends will suddenly discover that they have an extra few pounds of gear they absolutely must take to the top of Old Cattywampus Peak, and you'll be elected to carry it!

(By the way, 10 to 12 pounds is probably the most you'll ever need to carry in your day pack. Usually it will be much less. Water weighs a lot — 8 pounds to the gallon — so in hot weather your pack may be heavier because you'll be carrying more water.)

Besides being small, your day pack needs to be water resistant. Read the manufacturer's label to find out if it is. Most packs have a coating on the inside of the heavy-

duty nylon fabric. Check the inside of the pack. You should be able to see and feel the coating easily.

Many day packs have an upper and a lower compartment, but this isn't necessary. A single compartment is fine. Packs that zip shut and have a weather flap covering the zipper will keep your gear drier than drawstring packs.

The pack's shoulder straps should be padded and should have easily adjustable buckles. Try on the pack and test the buckles. A light waist belt of nylon webbing is nice but not absolutely necessary. The belt helps take some of the weight off your shoulders.

When you're looking for a day pack, don't forget to try on a "fanny" pack or two. As you can tell from the name, a fanny pack rests on your you-know-what. These handy packs have no shoulder straps. Instead, they have a belt

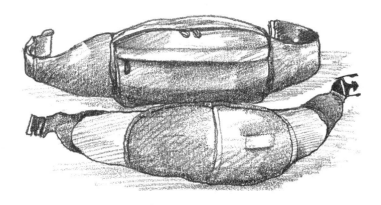

that goes around your waist. Some even have a handy holder for your water bottle. A fanny pack is especially good for short hikes when you don't have to carry a heavy jacket or lots of water.

Water container and water (musts). You need to take water on all hikes! In hot weather, take a quart for every 2 miles. When it's hot, drink water, not sweet drinks. Sweet drinks can make you feel thirstier.

In cold weather, take a pint for every 2 miles you're going to hike. If you don't mind the extra weight, hot chocolate in a thermos makes a mighty good snack in the winter. (But don't take hot chocolate *instead of* water. Take it *in addition to* water.)

Whether the weather's hot or cold, start drinking *before* you feel thirsty. Your "thirst indicator" doesn't start working until your body has already lost a lot of water. When you're hiking in hot weather, it's a good idea to drink at least a cup (8 ounces) of water every 20 to 30 minutes.

There are many different kinds of water containers for hiking — but none of them are glass! Some hikers like to carry one or two 1-quart or 1-liter plastic bottles. Others like to carry one or two small ones (1-pint or ½-liter), plus a larger one (or two) if the weather's warm. Plastic "canteens" are much lighter than metal ones.

Some water bottles can be attached to your belt or a belt loop. Some can be carried over your shoulder. All can

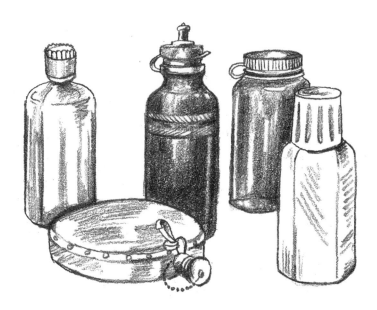

be carried in your pack. Wherever you put your water, be sure that the lid is on tightly and that the bottle is easy to get at while you're hiking.

It may seem strange to bring your own water on hikes along streams, rivers, and lakes, but there's a good reason for this. Nowadays, most water, even water in many "wild" places, is not safe to drink. Sometimes this is because cattle, sheep, or humans have polluted the water. Sometimes it's because poisons may have accidentally gotten into the water. Anyway, it's a good idea not to take any chances. Bring along *all* the water you think you'll need for a hike, unless you know for sure exactly where and when you're going to meet up with some safe water along the way (maybe at a friend's house or at a campsite with piped water). And even if you know there will be a safe water source, bring along some emergency water.

Comfortable, sturdy, well-broken-in shoes and thick, absorbent socks (both musts). If your feet have any sense, the first time you wear sandals, thin-soled shoes, or new shoes on a hike will probably be the last time! For day hiking, good-quality athletic shoes are fine. You don't really need hiking boots if you're not carrying a backpack or hiking on rough, rocky trails. If you haven't been doing much walking lately, bring along some pieces of moleskin for possible hot spots on tender feet. (Moleskin is like soft, thick adhesive tape that's fuzzy on top.)

Thick socks will help protect your feet from blisters, not to mention heat and cold. Avoid 100 percent cotton socks, because they get soggy and wrinkled, and this can cause nasty blisters. Some hikers swear by all-wool socks. Others like all-synthetic socks (orlon, polypropylene, nylon, and so on). And some like cotton-blend socks (about 50 percent cotton with wool and/or synthetics). Cotton-blend socks are especially good for keeping feet cooler in warm weather. All-wool and all-synthetic socks seem to keep feet warmer, so they're good for cool-weather hiking.

Food (a must). If you're going to be out hiking at lunchtime, be sure to bring along a good lunch. A sandwich or two, a few cookies, and a piece of fruit are easy to fix and to carry. Even on a short hike, be sure to bring along some high-energy snacks. Granola bars, trail mix, dried fruit, and nonmeltable candy and cookies are good choices.

Whole grains make good trail foods and snacks because they are higher in protein, fiber, vitamins, and minerals than white flour and other highly processed grains. "Enriched" flours have been processed to remove all these good-for-you (and good-tasting) things. A few vitamins have been put back in, which is why these processed flours and grains are called "enriched." Read labels carefully, because some "whole wheat" products have only a little bit of whole wheat in them. Look for "100%" whole wheat or whole grain on labels to make sure you're getting *all* whole grains.

Also look for trail foods and snacks that are sweetened with honey, date sugar, or fruit juices. These sugars are used by the body more slowly than regular white and brown sugar. This means you have more energy for a longer time.

Hat (a must). Wear something with a brim all around in hot weather. That way, you carry your own shade around with you all the time. When it's cold, wear something warm that covers your ears.

Wearing a hat is worth whatever little extra trouble it takes. Your head has many blood vessels in and on it in order to keep your brain well fed. This means it's easy for your brain to get overheated in summer and over-cooled in winter. When this happens, you start feeling awful and your brain doesn't work too well. (See pages 97–98 for more on the problems caused by getting too hot or too cold.)

Extra clothes (a must). Even in warm weather, you'll feel cool in a breeze if you're sweaty, so be sure to bring along a light jacket or sweater. When it's cool or cold, bring several layers of clothing. For example, you may start out with a long-sleeved shirt, sweater, light or heavy jacket, and windbreaker. As you warm up while hiking, you'll peel down, then layer up again when you stop. Don't forget gloves or mittens if it's cold.

For hot weather, all-cotton clothes are coolest. For cool or wet weather, a mixture of cotton and a synthetic fiber, wool, or all-synthetic fabrics are warmer and dry faster if they get wet. Wearing heavy, 100-percent cotton jeans or jean jackets is a mistake in wet weather. All-cotton fabrics take a *long* time to dry!

LAYERS COME OFF ⸻

Sturdy plastic or metal whistle (a must). It's a good idea to put the whistle on a nylon cord and hang it around your neck. Or attach the cord to your belt or a belt loop and put the whistle in your pocket. If there's an emergency and you need help, blow three short, loud blasts on the whistle every few minutes until help arrives.

Sunglasses and sunblock (musts). Sunglasses are a must for sunny summer *and* winter days. The sun's rays are likely to be strongest at higher altitudes (where there's less of the earth's atmosphere to protect you) or when there's snow on the ground (because snow reflects the sun back on you from all angles). Make sure your sunglasses filter out both UV-A and UV-B rays.

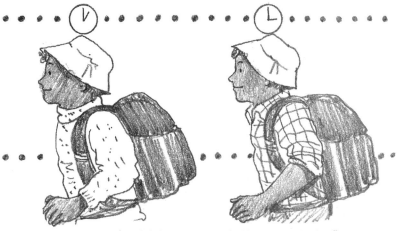

AS THE TEMPERATURE GOES UP.

Everyone should use a sunblock. An SPF ("sun protection factor") rating of 15 is a good choice for everyone except very fair people, who may need something with a higher rating. An SPF of 15 means that people who usually burn after being out in the sun for 20 minutes won't burn for 15 times 20 minutes (5 hours). If it takes you 10 minutes to burn, with SPF 15 you won't burn for 2½ hours. Remember to put sunblock on the tops of your ears and on your lips (use the stick kind for your lips).

Because you'll probably be sweating it off, put on more sunblock every couple of hours (more often if you burn easily).

Small flashlight (a must). It's a good idea to put your flashlight on a longish piece of nylon cord. Attach the cord to your belt or a belt loop and put the flashlight in your pocket when it looks like you'll be needing it soon. Otherwise, keep the flashlight in your pack. Don't forget an extra set of batteries and a bulb. (No disposable flashlights, please!)

Map and/or trail guide (a must). A map will not only tell you how to get from here to there, but also how to get back home again. (See pages 61–71 for information on maps.)

Watch (a must). Hikers wear or carry a watch so that they can make sure they are on schedule. It's no fun to miss your ride home or to finish a hike in the dark!

First aid kit (a must). As a beginner, you won't be expected to have a complete first aid kit. But even beginners need a basic kit. You could start out with an empty BandAid box. Put in several small and large BandAids, a couple of 2-inch by 3-inch nonstick adhesive bandages, several individually packaged moist towelettes, a tiny tube of first aid cream, and some pieces of moleskin that you've already cut into different sizes (don't forget to

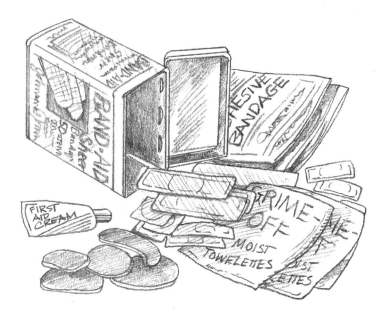

round the corners). These few items will help you handle small emergencies along the trail.

Your mini–first aid kit is just that — "mini." Your adult hike leaders will have much more complete first aid kits (and they'll know how to use them). Their kits might also include paper adhesive tape, large sterile dressings, a roll of 2-inch gauze, adhesive "butterflies" (for "stitching" wounds), aspirin (or another pain reliever), small scissors, pointed tweezers (for splinters, and so on), safety pins, antiseptic, insect repellent, an elastic bandage (for sprains and strains), "instant ice" (for bruises and sprains), and an American Red Cross sheet of emergency instructions. All these items should be in a waterproof container.

Most hikers develop their own list of first aid kit "musts" to add to the basics. Try to find out what items experienced hikers think are important to include in their first aid kits and begin a list of your own. You might also want to learn some first aid. Call the youth organizations in your town to find out if any of them offers a first aid course.

Coins for phone calls (a must). The money you bring for phone calls should be change, of course. Although you'll hardly ever need to make a phone call while on a hike, it'll make you feel better to know that you can if you want to. (In a serious emergency, you can dial "911" *without* coins. You can also call home "collect" without coins after dialing "O" for Operator.)

Small paper or plastic bag (very useful). Whether you're going around the block or around the world, "pack it in, pack it out" is the rule. Put all your garbage and litter in a bag, then empty the bag into a trash can. Keep the bag and use it again if you can. Whenever there's some extra room in your bag, fill it up with the litter left behind by careless hikers!

Bandanna (very useful). If you've never carried one before, you'll wonder how you ever got along without it. What do you use it for? A million and one things! For instance, tie it around your head to keep sweat out of your eyes. Use it as a tablecloth, napkin, or washcloth. Tie your keys and change in a corner of it. Wet it and cool yourself off by wiping your face and arms with it. Its uses are almost endless.

Large plastic garbage bag (very useful). You can use a bag like this to sit on if the ground is wet or damp. If it's raining, all you have to do is make holes for your head and arms, and you have a raincoat that will fit over you and your day pack. And of course you can always use the bag for trash!

Toilet paper (very useful). The most important thing to remember about used TP is to *pack it out!*

Notebook and pencil or pen (very useful). It's a good idea to keep these in a small plastic or other waterproof bag, just in case. Take a ballpoint pen, because it will have waterproof ink. You'll find all kinds of uses for these items. It's fun to make notes and sketches of things you see along the trail — landmarks, plants, animals, and so on. Some people even use them for playing games.

Binoculars and/or camera (for fun). A small pair of 7×35 binoculars is handy for spotting wildlife and looking up and down the trail. A small, easy-to-use camera will let you share your good times on the trail with family and friends.

When you start hiking you'll probably notice that the experienced adult hikers in your group have brought along some things that aren't on the list above. These items — for example, a pocket knife, waterproofed matches, and water purification tablets — are also "musts." However, they should be carried by the hike leaders, not by beginning hikers. As you become more trailwise, your hike leaders will show you how and when to use these essentials.

This may seem like a lot of gear to remember, but after a few hikes, you'll toss it all in your day pack almost without thinking. If you leave some of it in your pack all the time, it will take you only a few minutes to get ready for a hike.

A Backpacking Start-up List

When you've been hiking for a while and are in pretty good shape, you may want to try backpacking. As you might guess, *a backpacking gear list includes the items on your day-hiking gear list.* Because we've just talked about those items, they won't be repeated here. Instead, we'll talk about what you'll need to add to your list.

If you've been thinking that your day pack weighs about as much as you care to carry, don't panic as this list grows. As a beginner, you won't be expected to carry *everything* on the list! You won't be going out backpacking by yourself, so there'll be others along to share the load. And also keep in mind that all backpacking gear should be as lightweight as possible. Leave those heavy jeans, hardback books, and cassette players at home!

Backpack (a must). If you're going to be staying overnight along the trail, you'll need a backpack. These packs are larger than day packs, so you can carry the extra equipment needed for overnighting. When you're day hiking, you don't need a sleeping bag and pad, a tent, a stove, or much food. When you're backpacking, you do.

There are two main kinds of backpacks: ones with a frame that the pack hangs from (external frame) and ones with the frame inside the pack itself (internal frame). You won't know which kind is best for you until you try them both.

For your first few backpacking trips, it's a good idea to borrow a pack to try out. This way you can get an idea of which kind of pack is most comfortable for you. If you

EXTERNAL FRAME   INTERNAL FRAME

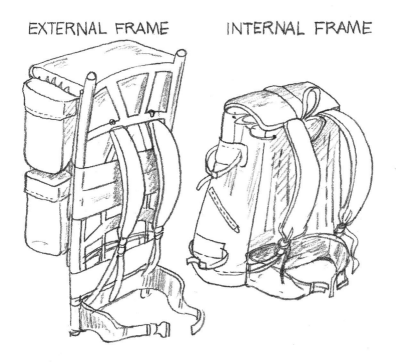

can't borrow a pack, you may be able to rent one from a store specializing in backpacking equipment. In any case, before you go on your first backpacking trip, try to talk with some experienced backpackers and find out what kind of equipment works best for them.

To rent or buy good-quality backpacking gear, it's a good idea to go to stores specializing in this kind of equipment. You can learn a lot about packs and other equipment by talking to the salespeople there (especially if they aren't too busy). If you find a pack that might be what you need, you can even ask a salesperson to put some weight in it so you can walk around the store and see if it's comfortable.

Of course, as a person with a smaller-than-adult body, you will need a smaller pack than some adults. Not all backpacking equipment stores carry smaller packs for young people. However, stores may carry packs that are made for smaller adult bodies. Most stores can order such packs, even if they don't usually carry them.

One of the first things you'll notice about a backpack (besides its frame) is that it has a padded hip belt. You need this padding because the weight of a backpack rests on your hips. Another thing you might notice right away is that backpacks usually have two main compartments and some outside pockets. These help you keep your gear organized. The leather "patches" on the outside of the pack bag are used for tying on pieces of gear — sleeping bags and pads, for example.

Backpack bags, like day packs, are usually made of heavy nylon materials that have been coated on the inside to make them repel water. Pack bags come in all colors and sizes. Some have lots of outside pockets and some don't. Some have straight zippers, some have curved zippers. Some are made to carry very heavy loads, some to carry light loads. When you finally decide to buy a backpack, you may find it hard to choose. But when you do choose, remember Old Cattywampus Peak.

Trail boots (a must). Good, sturdy, well-broken-in athletic shoes will work fine as long as you're carrying no

more than about 20 to 25 pounds. For heavier loads, back-packers usually need light- to medium- weight trail boots.

Light- and medium-weight trail boots have over-the-ankle tops and "lug" soles. (Lug soles look sort of like the bottom of a waffle iron. The lugs help you get a better grip on steep or rocky trails.) Trail boots may be made of leather or of leather and heavy nylon fabric.

It's a good idea to shop carefully for trail boots. Go to a specialty store, ask for some help, and try on several different kinds. First, put on a pair of lightweight inner socks (these should *not* be 100 percent cotton). Then, put on a pair of medium-weight wool or wool-blend socks. (This combination of socks is what most experienced hikers use on the trail.) Before you lace up the boots, push your foot forward until your toes touch the front of the boot.

You should be able to get your index finger between your heel and the back of the boot. Now lace up the boot — barely tight at the toes, tight on the top of your foot, not too tight at the top of the boot.

Next, spend about 20 minutes walking around on the store's carpets with both boots on. Scuff your foot forward hard so you can see if your toes will hit the end of the boot when you're hiking downhill (they shouldn't). Climb some stairs with just your toes, checking to see if your heel lifts more than 1/8 inch off the boot sole (it shouldn't). If the boot passes these tests and feels comfortable, you're in luck.

Be sure to break in your boots around town and on short day hikes for a few weeks before taking them out on a backpacking trip. If you don't, your feet will be sorry!

Sleeping bag, waterproof stuff sack, and nylon straps (musts). One of the things sleeping bags have in common with backpacks is that you need to check out a few before you'll know which one is best for you. Try to borrow or rent several different sleeping bags before buying one of your own.

The best sleeping bags for backpacking are filled with hollow, synthetic fibers (for example, Hollofill). Some sleeping bags are filled with goose or duck down (fine, soft feathers). The problem with down is that when it gets wet it all clumps together and can't insulate you anymore, so you get cold. And it can take a long time to dry and fluff up again when the weather's damp or wet. Hollow, synthetic fibers don't clump up when they get wet, so they still keep you warm. They also dry faster!

Most backpackers don't need a heavy sleeping bag when they take their trips during warm weather. A 3-pound bag is plenty warm enough for warm-weather backpacking. Most of a sleeping bag's weight is in the fill. The fabric on the outside should be lightweight ripstop nylon, nylon taffeta, or polyester and cotton fabric. All-cotton fabrics are heavy and take longer to dry when they get wet.

Another thing to look at is the seams. Make sure the bag's seams are not "sewn through." Sewn-through seams let cold air get too close to you. A bag with this kind of seam has plenty of cold spots. You can see why if you hold one up to the light. Try to find a bag with box-wall, slant-wall, v-tube, or double-quilt construction. A good bag will also have a nice, fat "draft flap."

Like backpacks, sleeping bags come in lots of colors and shapes. Look for a semi-mummy or barrel-shaped bag. Bags with these shapes weigh less than rectangular bags. Check the zippers, too. Your bag's zipper should be heavy, nonmetallic, and "two way." This means you'll be able to unzip it at the bottom and the top at the same time because there are two zipper heads — a handy option when you want to cool off your feet after a hard day's hiking!

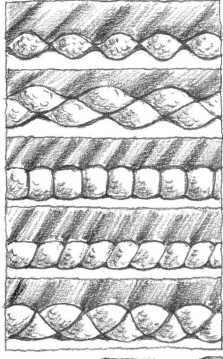

SEWN–
THROUGH

DOUBLE–
QUILT

BOX–WALL

SLANT–WALL

V–TUBE

RECTANGLE   BARREL   SEMI-MUMMY   MUMMY

When you're looking for a sleeping bag, remember that some bags made especially for young people aren't the kind you'll need for backpacking. That is, they may be great for slumber parties, but they may be sewn through and may not have "draft flaps" and heavy plastic zippers. However, a few manufacturers of high-quality sleeping bags do make some bags for smaller bodies. Look for them in backpacking specialty stores and catalogs.

To protect your sleeping bag from rain and dirt, you'll need a waterproof, nylon *stuff sack.* As the name implies, you just stuff your bag into the sack. This makes the bag easier to carry and cleaner (and drier) to sleep in. Look for stuff sacks of all sizes at camping supply stores.

And, unless your pack has a special sleeping bag compartment, you'll also need a pair of nylon straps for attaching your sleeping bag and pad to your pack. You can also find these just about anywhere camping supplies are sold.

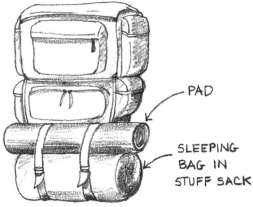

PAD

SLEEPING
BAG IN
STUFF SACK

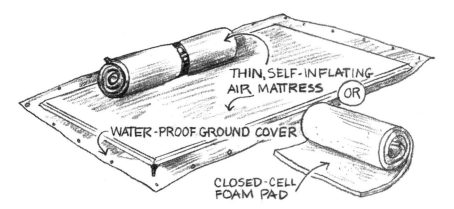

Pad and ground cover (musts). Whether or not you use a tent, you'll need a waterproof ground cover to put under the tent or under you and your pad. Many backpackers use a plastic *tube tent*; they're tough and lightweight and fold up small. And, of course, you can use a tube tent as a *tent* (see the picture on page 46) if your group is ever a tent short!

A pad will put a little distance between your bones and the hard (and sometimes cold) ground. To save weight, you can get a three-quarter-length pad and use your extra clothes under your other one-quarter. Be sure to get a *closed-cell* pad (⅜-inch thick is thick enough). This kind of pad doesn't absorb water. *Open-cell* pads are heavier, bulkier, and sop up water like a sponge!

Some backpackers prefer a thin, self-inflating air mattress. Compared to the old-fashioned air mattresses, these are light and easy to inflate. However, they are a lot more fragile than closed-cell pads (which don't deflate if they get a hole in them).

Many backpackers put their sleeping pad and ground cover in a stuff sack. Doing this keeps them together and makes them easier to attach to or put in a backpack.

Cup, spoon, and deep dish (musts). These three items will be the beginning of your kitchen kit. Later, as you become more experienced, you may add pots, a backpacking stove, and some fuel for the stove. Most campers use cups, spoons, and plates made of metal. Plastic is lighter, but it can crack—and if it gets too close to the stove....

DEEP DISH

CUP

SPOON

Tent (very useful; in some parts of the country, a must). When you start backpacking, you'll find there are folks who *always* use a tent, even when the weather's good. There are also people who *never* use a tent, even if the weather's bad. And there are those who sometimes use a tent and sometimes don't. Only you will be able to decide which kind of tent user (or nonuser) you'll be, but this will take time and a few backpacking trips.

If you'll be backpacking in areas that are usually cold, windy, or wet — even in summer — you may decide right away that a tent is a must. Even if this is true, as a backpacking beginner you probably won't be asked to provide a tent for a trip. Instead, you'll probably share a tent with more experienced backpackers.

If you'll be backpacking in places where the weather's mostly good, you may decide to sleep out under the stars on a ground cloth and pad. But even if you decide to do this, your leaders should make sure there are enough tents to go around if the weather turns bad.

Even if you won't need a tent at first, you can still start learning about them. The best backpacking tents are lightweight (3 to 4 pounds for one person, 5 to 6 pounds for two people), easy to put up (especially the poles), have head room (can you sit up?), shed water (is there a separate piece of water-repellent material over the top of the tent, called a *rainfly*?), and are movable before being staked down (can the tent stand alone after you put the poles in?).

Of course, there are other kinds of shelters besides tents with poles and rainflies. For instance, if it rains when you're planning to sleep out, you can put up your tube tent instead of using it for a ground cover. If you're using a tarp (a flat, waterproof piece of material) for a ground cover, you can make it into a lean-to or a pup tent with some nylon cord. It's fun — and a good idea — to practice putting up a lean-to and pup tent at home before going backpacking without a tent.

Rain gear (very useful). As mentioned in the day-hiking section, a big plastic garbage bag works pretty well. But if you'd like something a little snazzier, there's plenty to choose from. Some backpackers like a poncho that covers them and their pack. Others like to use a rain jacket and separate pack cover. The rain jacket should have a hood, of course, and a bill on the hood if you can get it. The bill helps keep rain from running into your face. Hikers who live in rainy parts of the country sometimes even wear rain pants. After a few trips, you'll know which kind of gear will be best for you.

Small trowel (very useful). This tool comes in handy at pit stops. Look for a hard plastic one (marked in inches or centimeters) at a camping supply store.

Books (for fun). Most backpackers are interested in what they see as they hike along the trail. Field guides can help you understand what you're seeing. There are paperback field guides for birds, flowers, trees, geology (rocks), stars, insects, animals, and more. See pages 158–159 for suggestions, then look them over at your local library or bookstores.

These are the "biggies" of basic backpacking equipment. Big in price, big in importance, and big in the fun you'll have using them. Of course, on any backpacking trip you take as a beginner your leader(s) will be bringing along other necessary items (water purification tablets and/or water filter, backpacking stove and fuel, cooking pots, pocket knife, "maxi" first aid kit, compass, insect repellent, pack repair kit, waterproofed matches, and so on).

Then, in addition to the basics we talked about above, there are a few other items you'll want to take along on most trips. For example, you'll need a toothbrush, comb, and small towel (a cloth diaper makes a fast-drying towel). You may also want to bring along a little hand lens and some travel games. These are things that make life on the trail more fun and more convenient. Now let's find out how to check out and pack up this gear!

Trial Runs

Before you go on a day hike or backpack into a wild area, it's a good idea to try out your gear at home. "Trial runs" are a good way to do this.

Checking out day-hiking gear. This is easy. Just get out a street map for your neighborhood and plot a course to some interesting point a mile or so away. A museum? A park? A backpacking equipment store? Mark your course with a colored pencil or pen. Be sure to check with your folks; tell them where you're going and when you'll be back. You could even call a friend or two to see if they'd like to go along. Then fix yourself some lunch or snacks,

put the gear we talked about in the day hiking section in your day pack (don't put your water bottle on top of your sandwich unless you want glop for lunch), and set off, map in hand.

After a few trial runs like this, you'll have your gear and your feet adjusted to the idea of hiking. Now talk some of your family and friends into going to the nearest place where there are some hiking trails (see the next section for ideas). Start with a hike of a couple of miles or so, and work your way up to more challenging ones. You're on your way!

Checking out backpacking gear. This takes a little more time. Let's assume that you've been day hiking for a while and are starting to get trailwise. You've talked some friends or family members who are experienced back-packers into taking a weekend backpack soon. They're going to bring tents and cooking equipment. You've even managed to borrow the basic gear you'll need. But you still don't feel ready.

Because you haven't backpacked before, you're a little worried about the details. How many pounds of gear should you carry, for instance? How do you put on a loaded pack? How should you roll your sleeping bag? You have your gear list, but you're not sure about where you should put things in the pack.

Well, one of the best ways to start figuring out these

kinds of details is to do a weekend backpacking trip right in your own backyard (or in your living room, if you don't have a backyard). Ask your backpacking friends for some advice. Many will suggest that it makes good sense to organize your gear (including clothes) in waterproof stuff sacks or in heavy plastic bags. Most of them will probably say that you should try to keep heavy items low in your pack, so you won't be top-heavy. They may also say you'll be more comfortable if you balance the weight evenly (left and right) and carry only about one-fifth of your body weight. This means pack, gear, food, water, clothes, and extras — everything! So, if you weigh 100 pounds, your total pack weight would be about 20 pounds.

Use your imagination. Sort your gear and put it in your pack. Put on your pack and walk around the block ten times. Keep adjusting your pack until it's comfortable. When you're hungry, stop and fix yourself something to eat. Clean up and repack your pack. Were things too hard to get at? Change your system and try again. When it gets dark, lay out your ground cloth (or put up a tent, if you have one), put down your pad and sleeping bag, make sure your pack (and food) are safe from animals, then go to bed. In the morning, get up and make breakfast. Clean up and repack. Hike around the block (or around town) some more. How are your feet doing? Do your shoes or boots need more breaking in? Are your water and snacks reachable? Can you put your pack on and take it off by yourself? When you've worked out answers to these kinds of questions, you'll be ready to go backpacking for real!

Where to Find Trails

For the kind of hiking and backpacking you're likely to do as a beginner, you'll need trails. (Very experienced hikers and backpackers often travel *cross-country* — that is, without trails. However, you need to know how to use a compass and maps, and to be in very good shape, before you try cross-country hiking.)

Luckily, there are trails almost everywhere: In the city. In the suburbs. In forests. Near beaches. Up mountains.

Down into canyons. Across the plains and the desert. Along rivers and creeks. Near your neighborhood and all over the world. This means that people who like hiking can have fun just about anywhere. In fact, sometimes a hiker's biggest problem is choosing where to hike next!

For information on trails close to (or in) your town or city, try calling or visiting the Chamber of Commerce, the Recreation Department, the library, and any parks you already know about. See "Where to Write for Trail Information" (page 168) and "Some Groups That Sponsor Hikes" (page 171) for more ideas.

When you start tracking down some trails you might like to try, you'll soon discover that certain places have lots of trails. City parks, for instance. State parks, too. And, of course, national parks such as Grand Canyon National Park (Arizona), Yellowstone National Park (Wyoming), and Shenandoah National Park (Virginia).

But parks aren't the only places where there are lots of trails. All over the United States are national forests, Bureau of Land Management areas, and wilderness areas. All of these lands are wildlands that have been set aside for public use.

Some wildland areas — state and national parks, for example — are allowed to have paved roads, visitor centers, large campgrounds, even restaurants and motels. Other wildlands, like the national forests, may have mostly dirt roads and very simple campgrounds. The wildest lands

of all, the wilderness areas, don't have any roads or campgrounds. But almost all wildlands have trails that are open only to hikers. (Some have horse trails, too.)

Take Only Pictures, Leave Only Footprints

Almost everywhere there are trails, there have to be a few rules to remind visitors about how to protect our wildlands. There may be different rules for different wild areas. You protect a desert a little differently from the way you protect a mountain meadow, for example. But most of the ways visitors can protect wildlands are just plain common sense. We'll talk about only a couple of reminders here — the two you're most likely to hear (or see) whenever you go hiking.

First, people are asked to "Pack it in, pack it out." There's no trash and garbage collection along the trail like there is in your neighborhood. Even if each visitor left only one bit of trash (and some leave a lot more than that!), our wildlands would soon be one big garbage dump. And who wants to get away from it all to a garbage dump? So hikers who really love wild areas take every last gum wad, candy wrapper, and bit of toilet

paper they bring with them back out again. Some hikers even pick up the trash careless visitors have left behind.

Another saying that helps hikers protect wild areas is "Take only pictures, leave only footprints." It's easy for most of us to see that if each visitor carried off an interesting rock or flower or pine cone or butterfly, soon all the "wild" would be gone from our wildlands. There wouldn't be much left to love about the mountains, the desert, or the seashore if we each took a bit of them home every time we visited (and left our trash behind).

These sayings are just common sense — and easy to remember, especially if you think of all the parks and forests and wilderness areas as being part of your backyard (even if you live in an apartment). You'd probably get mad if, when your friends visited you, they started walking through your yard, picking your flowers and vegetables, and tossing trash all over the lawn. And they'd get mad if you did the same things at their home.

So whenever you go hiking in wild areas, remember that these public lands are part of your and everyone else's backyard. And whether a wild area is a park, a national forest, or a wilderness area, it is first of all the home of living things of great beauty, interest, and importance. It is the home of wild animals and plants that depend on all of us to protect them from harm.

Now you're just about ready. But before you hit the trail, you'll need to master the basics of "wayfinding" and weather watching. The next chapter will help you do just that!

2
Reading Maps — and the Weather

"Wayfinding" and weather watching are a couple of fun (and essential) trail skills you'll want to practice up on before you ever hit the trail. You can actually practice them just about anywhere. Weather, you'll certainly agree, is everywhere — including your neighborhood. And no matter where you live, you can probably find maps of that place. So here are a few suggestions to help you learn more about maps and weather — starting close to home.

Finding Your Way

When you're a beginning day hiker and, later, a beginning backpacker, you'll mostly be walking on paths made especially for hiking. Of course, you may sometimes hike on sidewalks, paved roads, gravel roads, or dirt roads. But no matter what kind of "trail" you hike on, you'll need a map to help you get where you want to go — and back again. (After you're more trailwise, you'll probably learn how to use a compass, too.)

Different Kinds of Maps

One kind of map you may already be familiar with is a street map of the town you live in. Another kind you may have used is a map of your state. And then there are the maps of the United States and the world that you've probably studied at school. But there are many other kinds of maps, too.

Park maps. When you're going hiking in wild areas, you need maps that show the trails. There are many different kinds of trail maps. The ones you find at your city park or regional park may be very simple. For example, these maps may show only the trails themselves, a few landmarks (such as a paved road or building), and the distances between some points.

At a national park, like Denali (Alaska) or Everglades (Florida) the visitor center will probably have some simple maps and some detailed maps. The more detailed maps may show where to see different kinds of plants and animals, how high the hills and mountains are, and even how long it can take to hike from one place to another.

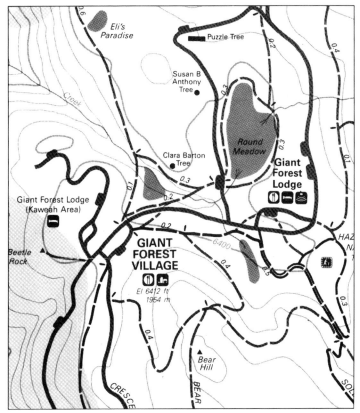

National Park Map

National forest and Bureau of Land Management (BLM) maps. If you go hiking in a national forest or BLM area, you'll discover that maps can be very large! (Many are about 30 by 30 inches.) They also have lots of details. Both national forest and BLM maps show many different

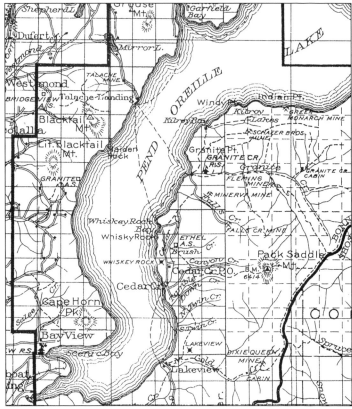

National Forest Map

kinds of roads and trails. You may be surprised at the
number of roads there are in national forests. Many of
these roads are used by logging trucks to carry trees to
lumber mills outside the forests.

Besides showing roads and trails, BLM maps often tell you what kind of activities different areas are good for. These maps also include information on campgrounds, interesting natural areas, and scenic places. Lands managed by the BLM, like national forest lands, aren't just for hiking-type recreation. For example, mining for many different kinds of minerals is allowed on BLM lands.

National forest and BLM maps also show some *elevations* — the number of feet a place is above sea level. The maps also use different colors to indicate who manages the lands. For instance, a medium green is usually used for national forest land, orange for BLM land, a lilac color for state land, and yellow for Native American land. Somewhere in the mapfolder, you may also find a few paragraphs on where to camp and where to find water.

Topographic maps. These are the kind of maps most experienced hikers use. *Topo* comes from the Greek word meaning "place" and *graphia* from the Greek word for "to write." So topographic maps (or "topos," as they are usually called) are "written records of places."

Topographic maps show more than just trails, roads, lakes, rivers, buildings, forests, and so on. In addition to all these details, they show the ups and downs of a certain area, so hikers can tell how hard or easy a trail is going to be. The *contour lines* help tell you not only

whether the land goes up or down but how *steeply* it goes up or down. If the lines are close together, the land is steep. If they are very far apart, the land may be almost flat. The numbers you see right along some contour lines are elevations (the number of feet the land is above sea level).

Where can you get topo maps? One source could be your local backpacking specialty store. Some national and state parks also sell them at their visitor centers. However, because it takes hundreds of topo maps to cover the whole country, most stores and parks have only the ones for their region.

The best source for topo maps for anywhere in the United States is the U.S. Geological Survey (USGS). The USGS is the government bureau that gathers the information and prints the topo maps. If you don't know which topos you'll need, write to the USGS (see page 170 for addresses) and ask for a guide to reading topo maps, as well as an order form and a map index for the state you want to hike in. The guide and index are free, and the maps are not expensive.

Once you've found a source for topo maps, you'll need to decide between a *15-minute map*, which covers an area of about 13 by 17 miles, or a *7½-minute map*, which covers an area of about 6½ by 8½ miles. As a beginning hiker taking short hikes, you'll probably choose the second kind. (Map *minutes*, by the way, are measures of space, not time. There are 60 minutes in a *degree*, and one degree covers about 70 miles of latitude or longitude at the equator.)

Learning How to Use Maps

A good way to start becoming familiar with the kind of maps you'll be using for hiking is to read all the fine print on one. Begin by looking for the arrow that indicates which way is north on the map (all good maps have this arrow). Now look for the *scale*, which shows you how many inches or centimeters represent a mile or kilometer on that particular map. The scale of a map depends on how much area the map covers. On a state map, for instance, 1 inch might equal about 20 miles (32.2 kilometers). On a county or national forest map, 1 inch might equal 5 miles (8 kilometers). And on a topo map, an inch might cover just ½ mile (⅘ kilometer). (You won't actually use state or county maps for hiking, but they do come in handy for figuring out how to get to nearby — or faraway — hiking places.)

SCALE

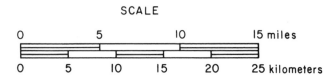

LEGEND

▬▬▬	National Forest Boundary
③	State Highway
🔢 12	Forest Highway
0950	Forest Development Road
+—+—+—+	Railroad
🚩	Supervisors Headquarters
🚩	District Ranger Station
🚩	Guard or Ranger Station not permanently occupied

Report fires here

Next, look for the map's *legend*, which tells you what the symbols on the map mean. By looking carefully at the legend, you'll be able to tell a two-lane road from a freeway, and a dirt road from a trail. The legend may include symbols for airports, roadside rests, mines, parks, and campgrounds.

Some maps also tell you how many miles it is from one place to another — usually from one city to another or one road junction to another.

But what about trails? Do topo maps, national forest maps, and BLM maps tell you how many miles (or kilometers) it is from one place to another on a trail? Well, they do and they don't. You won't find the mileages right next to the trail on these maps. Instead, you must check the scale and then measure the parts of the trail you want to hike. One way to do this is to take a few inches of thin

string or heavy thread and mark it with a pen in ½-mile pieces. Then lay the string along the trail. (Most trails aren't straight, which is why the string is handy.) By counting the marks, you can get an idea of how far it is from one place to another.

If you're using a topo map, it's also a good idea to figure out how much the trail goes up and down. After you've been using topo maps for a while, you'll find it easy to see the hills and valleys, canyons and mountaintops. In a while you'll have learned how to orient the map using unusual land features like steep cliffs, dry streambeds, water sources, and even buildings. Eventually, when you look at a topo map, it'll seem almost three-dimensional!

Reading the Trail

Hikers need maps, and they need to know how to use them. But they also need something else that they always have with them, something they can't leave behind or forget — their senses. If you learn to pay attention to the information your eyes and ears and nose and skin are always giving you, you probably won't lose your way. There may be times when you're not quite sure where you are — whether you're 2 miles or 3 miles from the last trail junction, for example. But that's not the same thing as losing your way or being lost.

Most of the time, people aren't paying much attention to what's going on around them. Oh, they may know whether it's raining or not, but they probably can't tell you the color of the cars they've just passed on the street. This is OK when you're in familiar territory. Not knowing the color of the cars isn't going to keep you from finding your way home. There are lots of familiar things along the way to keep you on track.

On the trail, though, it's usually different. Unless you've hiked a trail several times, there won't be much that's familiar about it. And although many trails in parks,

national forests, and wilderness areas have signs that tell you how far it is to the next trail junction or place of interest, you still need to become a good observer. You need to make seeing things along the trail a habit.

It helps to take notes in your head (or on a piece of paper, if the route is complicated) as you walk along. Your notes might sound something like this: "Let's see, this trail starts at that big oak tree, then crosses this little bridge made of three logs. Now it goes across and up this hill toward that big pine tree. When I stop and look back I see two big rocks with the road behind them. Now we're at the top of the hill. From here, I can see...." You get the idea.

As you're making these notes, stop occasionally to check your map and match up the hills, valleys, rock piles, and streams the map shows with what you're seeing. Notice where these landmarks are in relation to each other, to the trail, and to you. What's the name of that peak over there? Is the trail going to cross that stream you can see in the distance? Pencil in an arrow on the map showing where you are and which way you're facing. Now make a simple sketch in your notebook (or on

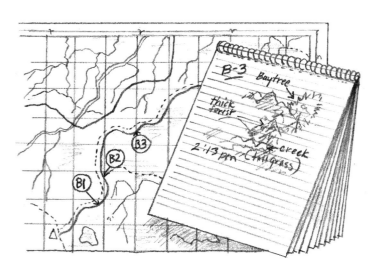

the map) of the landmarks you can see. Don't forget to label the sketch.

Taking mental notes and making sketches (even when you're hiking around town) helps you to get into the habit of noticing and remembering your surroundings. This skill comes in handy when you're in unfamiliar territory and need to retrace your steps. By paying attention to what's all around you, you'll know where you are, where you've been, and where you're about to be. When this becomes a habit, you'll find you're storing up all kinds of interesting and wonderful hiking memories.

What to Do If You *Do* Lose Your Way

Although nobody ever plans on getting lost, it does happen. It can happen to anyone. That's why it's a good idea to know how to get "found" again. Getting found, you'll be happy to know, is almost as easy as getting lost — but not quite. To get found, you need to pay attention to what you're doing (which is what you *didn't* do when you lost your way).

You'll know you've lost your way when you can't figure out how to get back to where your group is or where you started from. When this happens, STOP. Don't go any farther. Right away, get out your whistle and blow three good, loud blasts. (Three of anything — shouts, whistle blasts, bright-colored pieces of gear — means "help." Two of each means "I/we hear you.") If your group is still near you — and they should be — they'll hear you. Soon you'll all be together again.

Suppose, though, that you really haven't been paying attention for quite a while. Your group may not have missed you yet and may have gone a long way down the trail. They may be too far away to hear your whistle. If, after you blow several sets of three blasts, your group doesn't answer, sit down in a sheltered place. Have a snack and a drink and try to figure out where you are. Every once in a while, blow some more sets of three blasts.

If you're still not sure where you are, stay put. Don't go anywhere unless you are *sure* that you've figured out where you are. Even if it's late in the day and you have to spend a night outside with only the basics in your day pack, you'll be OK. After all, your group isn't going to go home without you. They may have to get other people to help find you, and that may take a while. But they'll find you — *if* you stay where you are and don't wander even farther off from where you were supposed to be, and if you keep blowing those three blasts on your whistle pretty often.

Reading the Weather

Weather "reading" is a lot different from map reading. You can't write away for a weather "map" or pick one up at the store. What you can do, though, is be on the look-out for certain weather signs. Once you get in the habit of paying attention to these signs, you'll have some idea — some of the time — of what the weather is likely to be for a day or two and/or whether it's likely to change soon.

Of course, you'll only be right *some* of the time. Even professional weatherpeople aren't right about the weather *all* of the time. Because it's so hard to predict the weather, it's not surprising that hikers sometimes find themselves out on a cold, muddy trail when they'd rather be home eating popcorn in a nice, warm living room. But

although you won't *always* be able to stay dry (or cool or warm) while hiking, there are some things you can learn that will help keep you out of weather trouble a lot of the time.

Check the Weather Reports

One thing that experienced hikers start doing several days before they go on a trip is read and listen to weather reports for the area they'll be hiking in. Because weather often changes quickly, however, there's no need to call off your trip if the weather is bad for a few days before. Keep your eyes and ears on the weather reports right up until you're ready to leave.

If you're going to hike somewhere near your home and the weather looks good even though the reports are bad, you might as well give the trip a try — if it's a day trip. If the trip is for overnight or longer, the experienced hikers in your group should decide whether or not to go ahead.

Watch the Weather While Hiking

The weather usually gives you some clues about what it's likely to do next, so be on the lookout for them. Most weather clues have to do with clouds, winds, and humidity (the amount of dampness in the air).

Different kinds of clouds. Anyone can learn to "read" some of the most important messages clouds have to give. The first thing cloud watchers should know is that there are three main kinds of clouds. The pillowy, billowy, sort of solid-looking clouds are called *cumulus* clouds. Layered-looking clouds are called *stratus* clouds. And wispy, turned-up-at-the-end clouds are called *cirrus* clouds.

Big, white, solid-looking cumulus clouds usually mean good weather. Sometimes, though, these clouds can darken and turn into anvil-shaped *thunderheads*. When they do this, look out — thunder, lightning, and rain may be on the way!

Flat, layered stratus clouds often produce nothing more than hazy sun. But if they start thickening up quickly and get heavy enough to block out the sun, there's a chance they may drizzle on you. If they also turn dark and drop down low, they may even rain out your hike. Just keep your eye on them.

It's easy to see why the wispy cirrus clouds are sometimes called "mare's tails." Often these clouds will only

whisk across the sky, making interesting patterns. Occasionally they may thicken up, get lower, and rain on you. See if you can figure out which they're going to do.

Wind and calm. If you know something about what happens when temperatures go up and down, winds aren't quite so mysterious. Because hot air is lighter than cold air, hot air rises and cold air "falls." When hot and cold air change places, wind is created. But that's only part of the story. It doesn't help you figure out when it's going to be too windy to hike.

Listening to and reading the weather reports is one way to get an idea about when the weather's going to be *really* windy. You can also do some cloud watching (if you're going to be hiking close to home). When clouds are moving rapidly across the sky, the weather may be changing quickly. If the temperature is dropping and the clouds are getting darker and lower, look out! If the temperature is rising and the clouds are getting higher and fewer, start packing your pack!

Water in the air. Humidity, mist, fog, drizzle, rain, sleet, hail, snow — for the most part, these are not the hiker's friends. (Though rain can be nice when the weather's been very hot and dry, and snow can be welcome if you're waiting for a chance to go "hiking" on that new pair of cross-country skis!)

When it's not raining and you're not exercising, but your clothes and skin feel warm, damp, and sticky, it's *humid*. In other words, there's a lot of water in the air. If it's getting stickier and stickier, check the other weather signs. It may be about to rain.

Some parts of the country are much foggier and mistier than others. Fog and mist can mean trouble for hikers. When it's foggy, you may not be able to see landmarks. Sometimes you may not even be able to see the trail more than a few feet ahead.

If your group plans to hike in an area where it gets foggy often (such as near the ocean), you and your leaders should talk with hikers who are familiar with the area about when and where to look out for fog and mist. In most places, they form at certain times of the day — such as early morning or late evening. Learn all you can, so that if it turns foggy while you're hiking you and your leaders will be prepared.

A little drizzle doesn't keep most hikers off the trail. But a long, hard rain usually doesn't improve a hiking trip, especially if thunder and lightning tag along. Watch the weather signs, and take along rain gear if you're in doubt.

If thunder and lightning do catch up with you on the trail, take shelter near the lowest, dry objects around you. Never hang around the highest trees, rocks, or hills. Don't go into a building that's all by itself with no higher objects near it.

Hailstorms are hard to predict. In many areas, they're most likely to occur during changing spring weather. Luckily, they usually don't last long. If your group gets caught in one, try to get under some kind of shelter (even bushes will do).

What about heavy snow and sleet? For now, stay away from them while hiking. Until you're out of the beginning hiker and backpacker stage, you're likely to enjoy hiking more (and be safer) if you take trips in warmer weather.

Amateur Weather Forecasting

Weather's a very tricky subject, but there are a few weather happenings that can help hikers forecast what's in store for them along the trail.

For instance, the weather's probably going to be good if you notice the following:

- a yellow sunset or sunrise
- a clear horizon at sunrise or sunset
- a cloudless sky, only a few clouds, rising clouds, or high clouds going in one direction
- fog and mist that burn off early
- gentle winds

The weather may be about to take a turn for the worse when you notice the following:

- a red sunset or sunrise
- a gray horizon at sunrise or sunset
- a ring around the sun or moon
- thunder and/or lightning nearby
- black clouds on the horizon, or clouds getting lower and moving in different directions
- a sudden drop in temperature and increasing winds

Weather, of course, is constantly changing. Paying attention to weather is an important — and fun — part of every hiking trip. In fact, you may discover that you'll remember a lot of hikes in terms of what the weather was like at the time. For example, you may find yourself recalling "the hike when the wind blew Martha's hat down the canyon," or "the one where Matt got that great shot of the rainbow over Old Cattywampus Peak." And bad weather doesn't necessarily mean a bad hiking trip — you may even notice that some hikers' favorite trip stories feature weather wonders! Anyway, if you keep your eye out for the weather signs mentioned above, you probably won't be unpleasantly surprised by the weather very often.

Now it's finally time to hit the trail!

3
On the Trail

When you're walking around town, perhaps going to the store or the library, you usually don't think about stopping to rest or being thirsty. You probably aren't thinking about food (unless you're on your way to get some) or about how fast you're walking (unless you're late). On the trail, it's different. You do need to think about these things, especially at first. Later, when you've become more trailwise, you'll take care of these things almost automatically.

Trail Walking

When you start hiking, you'll find that each person has her or his own pace and rhythm. Some walk fast (though they may poop out soon if they're not in good shape). Some walk slowly (they may be looking at the scenery, or

they may be out of shape). Some walk steadily (they usually aren't super-tired at the end of the day). And some are always speeding up and slowing down (they may want to be first but often wind up last — and very tired).

Most experienced hikers walk steadily, using a stride that is comfortable for them. They may walk fast, slow, or medium, but they don't sprint or creep. Trailwise hikers know that hiking is hiking — not a race to see who can get to the trail's end first!

Sometimes the group you're hiking with will have a few fast hikers and a few slow hikers. This can make it hard to keep the group together — which is important, so that no one is left behind. You can make sure no one gets left by slowing the group's pace, stopping more often, and having the slowest hikers walk in the middle of the

line. When you're backpacking, the fastest hikers can carry more of the group's "community" gear, like cooking pots, stoves, fuel, tents, food, and so on. Some extra weight will slow the sprinters down a little.

When the trail goes up a steep hill, many hikers shorten their stride and use the *rest step*. To do this, just pause for a second or two after you've swung a leg forward and have put it on the ground. That is, pause before you put your full weight on the leg. This will give it a little rest. When you go up a hill this way, you'll feel less tired at the top. It also helps to breathe more deeply when you find yourself huffing and puffing up a hill.

Hikers usually look forward to going downhill. But your toes and knees won't thank you if you go downhill too fast or for too long. So relax your knees (don't lock them), enjoy cooling down, look around you, and don't hurry on the downhill parts of a hike.

When the weather's hot, hike at a slow pace. Stop in the shade often for short rests and long drinks. Don't push yourself — heat exhaustion is no fun. (See pages 97–98 for what to do when hikers get overheated.)

Soon, if you hike regularly, you'll figure out the right hiking pace and rhythm for you. And you'll know you're getting trailwise and in good shape when you find yourself sweating up a hill and working hard, but still enjoying the scenery, talking with the other hikers, and feeling perfectly comfortable.

Trail Munching and Drinking

Munching is already likely to be one of your favorite things to do. On the trail, though, the best munchies may not be quite the same as your everyday ones. For instance, it's a good idea to avoid super-sugary, meltable snacks like chocolate bars. Instead, try some trail mixes. One trail mix that's been around for a long time is GORP ("grand old raisins and peanuts"). Some newer mixes are made of dried fruits (bananas, dates, raisins, and/or papaya), nuts (peanuts, walnuts, cashews, and/or pecans), coconut, honey-crisped oats, and sometimes even candy-coated chocolate. Some people make their own trail mix.

Many hikers "graze" their way up and down the trails.

A few eat only at mealtimes. As a beginning hiker, you'll probably feel livelier if you snack often. There's no need to stop while you snack if you've put your munchies where you can reach them without taking off your pack. Many hikers put snacks in several pockets!

Another way to keep your energy up is to drink, drink, drink. Because the human body's thirst indicator is a little slow to kick in, you'll need to drink *even when you are not thirsty.* As you go down the trail, imagine a sign dangling in front of you, like a carrot on a stick. The sign says "DRINK!" In hot weather, drink at least a cup of water every 20 to 30 minutes. In cool weather, you can drink a little less often.

If you don't drink, you'll soon feel tired (maybe exhausted), sickish to your stomach, headachy, and even dizzy. Hiking will not be fun. You'll wish you had never come — all because you didn't DRINK!

Be sure to keep your water bottle where you can reach it without taking off your pack. Hook it on your belt. Put an extra bottle in a reachable outside pocket of your pack if you're backpacking. (Remember that water bottles for hiking should always be unbreakable — no glass!)

What should you be drinking? The answer to that is easy — water. When you sweat, you sweat water. Water is what you need to put back into your body. If you absolutely must have some flavor to your water, make your flavored drink very weak. For example, if you like fruit juice, use one cup of juice and three cups of water. Do the same for any sugary drink. Sugary drinks may taste good going down, but they'll actually make you thirstier.

On day hikes, you'll be able to bring along all the water you'll need for the day. On backpacking trips, this will be harder. Water is heavy; a gallon weighs eight pounds! Your pack will be too heavy to carry comfortably if you bring along all the water you need for two days or more. In other words, you may have to use water from streams, springs, or lakes. This sounds easier than it is, though.

In most parts of the country, water isn't too hard to find. What is hard to find is water that's pure enough for people to drink. Because there are so many hikers using wild places now, a lot of water sources aren't safe to drink from anymore. The water may have bacteria or viruses in it that can make you quite sick.

Luckily, there are several ways hikers can "treat" water to make it safe to use. Some backpackers boil their next day's supply of water each night. How long you boil the water depends partly on the altitude you're at. The higher you are, the longer you have to boil it. At sea level, 10 minutes is usually long enough. Because the extra stove fuel needed to do this adds weight to a backpack, many hikers use other methods to purify water.

One of the other methods of purifying water is to treat it with tablets containing iodine. This takes about 15 to 30 minutes, depending on how cold the water is. The colder the water, the longer purification takes. Also, don't be surprised if iodine-containing water treatment tablets make the water taste funny. (But better a funny taste than getting sick!) Look for the tablets at backpacking specialty stores and drugstores.

These specialty stores may also have the small water filters some hikers use for purifying their water. The best filters have a very tiny pore size for removing the tiniest illness-producing organisms. They are also easy to use. (Some of the earliest filters didn't do a good job of getting

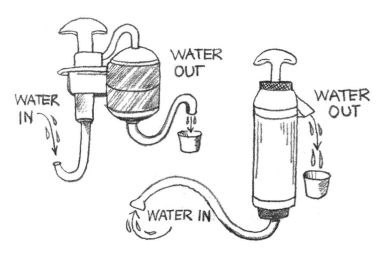

TWO KINDS OF WATER FILTERS

out all the disease organisms; they also took a lot of muscle to use.) Good filters aren't cheap, though they are not as expensive as they used to be.

Be sure to watch carefully whenever the experienced hikers in your group are treating water. You'll soon see that no matter which method your group uses, it's not hard to make water safe to drink.

Rest Stops Along the Trail

It's a good idea for beginning hikers to take a short rest every 20 to 30 minutes, or even more often if the trail is steep. While you're resting, take a drink. Munch. Look around you. Are there flowers blooming? Is there a view of distant mountains or plains, animals, or important landmarks? Check your map. Take a picture or make a quick sketch.

How long should a rest stop be? Long-time hikers say 5 to 7 minutes should do it. This is about how long it takes for your muscles to get rid of most of the waste products that make them feel tired. If you rest longer or rest too often, you stiffen up. Then it's hard to get going again.

When you stop for a meal, make it a light one. If you eat a lot, quite a bit of your blood will hang around your stomach for an hour or so. This means that your muscles won't have much to work with. You may feel sleepy or tired, and you probably won't feel like hiking.

If the weather's cool, be prepared to whip out a sweater or a jacket at rest stops. You may be toasty warm while hiking, but when you stop (especially if there's a breeze) you may start feeling cold. (See page 98 for what to do when hikers get too cold.)

Watch Out!

Hikers never enjoy getting blisters, being too hot or too cold, getting poison ivy or poison oak, being bitten or stung by insects, getting sunburned, being bruised in a fall, feeling sick to their stomach, having a headache, or getting so tired they don't know how they're going to make it home.

You'll be happy to know that almost all these nasty things can be avoided. Because accidents can occur anywhere — on the trail or at home — even trailwise hikers sometimes have bad luck. But most accidents don't need to happen, if you think ahead. Here are a few things you can think ahead about.

Blisters. Hike only in well-broken-in athletic shoes or hiking boots. When day hiking, wear thick, absorbent socks. (See page 23 for advice on choosing socks.) When backpacking, wear two pairs of socks (a thin inner sock to carry sweat away from your skin and a medium-weight, part-wool outer sock).

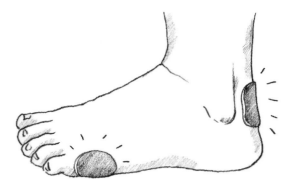

If you're hiking and a spot on your foot starts to feel "hot," stop. Take off your shoe and sock. Put a piece of moleskin (see page 23) on the hot spot. Now you probably won't get a blister. Next time you go hiking, put moleskin on the sensitive place before you start.

If you do get a blister, ask someone who knows first aid to treat it for you. The first-aider may sterilize a needle, let the fluid out of the blister, and then cover it with moleskin.

Being too hot or too cold. If hikers get too hot while hiking in warm weather, they may get *heat exhaustion*. When you feel faint and sick to your stomach and your skin is pale and sweaty, you may have heat exhaustion. Immediately lie down in a shady place, drink water, and rest. After you're feeling well again, you can continue hiking — slowly. And keep drinking lots of water.

A more serious misery is *heatstroke*. People with heatstroke usually have red faces. Their skin is hot and *dry*. This is because they have gotten so hot their body isn't working right. They've stopped sweating, so evaporation can't cool them. Their body temperature is getting higher and higher. They need to be cooled off very quickly. If there's cool water nearby, put them in it or pour water over them. If there is no water nearby, have them lie down flat in the shade and fan them. Send for help right away!

At the other end of the scale are shivering hikers. Whenever you start shivering, you may be on your way to *hypothermia*. This rather long word just means that your body temperature is lower than it should be. When this happens, you can get confused, stumble, feel miserable, and possibly have a serious accident. If you start feeling chilly while hiking, get out of the wind and/or rain, add more layers of clothes, and have a snack. If you still can't get warm, ask more experienced hikers for help.

The sun. Whether it's hot or cold, you can get a sunburn. If you're a few thousand feet above sea level, it's even easier to get a burn. At higher altitudes, there is less of the earth's atmosphere to protect you from the sun's rays. Today, however, there's no excuse for getting a sunburn. All you need to do is use some sunblocking lotion.

Creatures that bite or sting. All you can do about bees, wasps, and yellow jackets is try to stay out of their way. Mostly, if you don't bother them, they won't sting you. Mosquitoes and other small biters are another story. (Did you know that most "biters" are really suckers?) Bug repellent with 50 percent "DEET" in it works well for many of these little pests. (DEET is a chemical that many, but not all, biting insects hate.) Using a lotion with *more* than 50 percent DEET won't give you any more protection than the 50 percent kind.

In the southwestern United States, hikers usually keep an eye out for poisonous scorpions and rattlers. Scorpions sting and rattlers bite. But they won't do either of these to

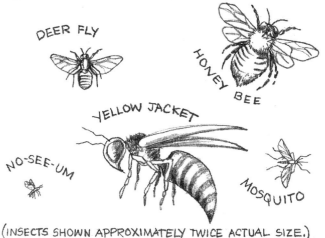

(INSECTS SHOWN APPROXIMATELY TWICE ACTUAL SIZE.)

you if you just keep your eyes open and your hands (and other parts of you) out of places you can't see into. Although rattlers, scorpions, and a few other animals can be dangerous, they are also beautiful in their own way. Enjoy them from a respectful distance. Remember, too, that they're all important parts of our world's ecosystems.

Unfriendly plants. There's an old rhyme that goes "leaves of three, let it be." Do it — especially if the leaves

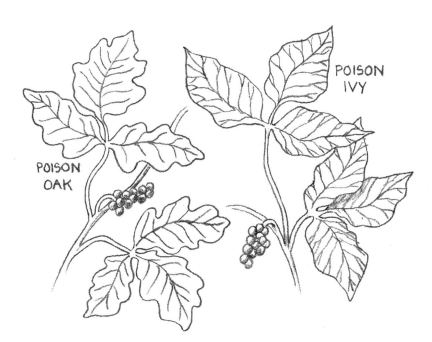

are shiny. If you've accidentally gotten into poison oak or poison ivy, run cold water over the skin that has touched the leaves as soon as possible. Also wash your clothes (by themselves) with soap and hot water as soon as possible. It's the plant's oil that causes the rash (it's also what makes the leaves shiny). Washing will get rid of most of it.

Nettles are common in many parts of the United States. Try not to brush them with your bare skin if you see them along the trail. If you do, the sharp little hairs on their leaves will give you a mild rash. It usually lasts only a few hours.

Altitude (mountain) sickness. Nearly anyone can be a victim of altitude sickness, even people who are in good shape. But trailwise hikers know better than to start hiking right after they've gone from sea level to above 4,000 feet. If you live near sea level, you need some time to get used to the thinner air of higher altitudes. Whenever you plan a hike above 4,000 feet, allow time to get used to less oxygen. You can do this by getting there the night before. By the next morning, you should be ready to hike at 4,000 to 7,000 feet.

If you don't allow enough time to get used to the altitude or if you hike too fast, look out. Hikers who do this often wind up feeling sick to their stomach, headachy, super-tired, and generally miserable. The best thing for them to do is to go back down to a lower elevation. This usually means that the whole group will have to go down. It pays to plan ahead so this doesn't happen to you.

Treating Trails (and Other Hikers) Right

At home, people get along better and enjoy life more when everyone does his or her share. You put trash in the trash can and dirty clothes in the hamper. You don't trample the plants in the flower and vegetable gardens.

It's not much different along the trail. But just as you had to learn what to do at home as you grew up, you have to learn what to do along the trail. As we mentioned in Chapter 1, responsible hikers "take only pictures and leave only footprints." That is, they try to *leave no trace* on the land they hike through. This kind of hiking and backpacking is called "low impact." Here are a few low-impact pointers for you to follow.

Stay on the trail. Trails are there for you to hike on. They are expensive to build and hard to maintain. You can help by hiking only on the trail. There'll be times when you'll want to take a shortcut, especially when the trail is zigzagging — but please don't do it. When people take shortcuts all over the place, soon it's impossible to

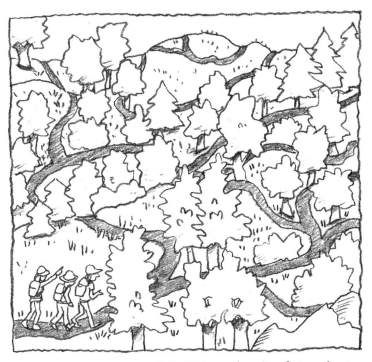

tell where the main trail is. This makes it a lot easier to get lost.

Also, when it rains, the water washes away the trail wherever the edges have been trampled. A single trail leaves most of the land in good health. Shortcutting can quickly destroy a beautiful area.

Pack it in, pack it out. This means everything, including toilet paper and chewed-over gum!

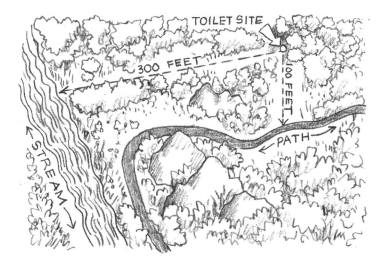

Give a hoot, don't pollute. If there are no toilets near your trail, walk at least 100 feet (50 paces) from the trail — 300 feet from any water source — before using an outdoor, "do-it-yourself" toilet. Take someone with you or make sure you can still see the trail and your group.

For solid wastes, use a sharp rock or small trowel to dig a shallow hole. After you've finished, cover up the wastes with the dirt you just dug out. If there are leaves or loose rocks, put some on top of the dirt. Imitate nature. Try to make the place look the same as it did before. *Do not bury toilet paper.* Put it in your litter bag and take it with you.

Respect life. The outdoor world may look as if you can't hurt it, but you can. When you stop to rest, try to find some flat rocks, a sandy or gravelly place, or a place that has more dirt than plants. (A squashed plant is usually a dead plant.) Admire flowery meadows from the trail. Meadows are very fragile and take a long time to heal after people have trampled them.

Hike in small groups. It's easier to get to know and keep track of hikers in a small group (two to eight people). Large groups are hard on the land; small ones are easier on it. A small group needs only a little space to rest and camp in. Fewer people also mean less trampling of plants and less disturbance of animals. A bonus is that you're more likely to see wildlife if your group is small and quiet.

Help keep it wild. A "walk on the wild side" isn't anything like a "wild party." At a party, you expect noise, music, and a fair amount of just plain running around. On a hike into wild country, the noises and music people expect to hear are the wind in the trees, the rustle of grasses, the songs of birds, and the rush of running streams and rivers. When hikers meet others along the trail, they may stop and talk. Because they go hiking to enjoy wild country, though, considerate hikers "keep it wild" by talking and walking quietly. And they never bring along radios or cassette players! This way, all hikers can enjoy the wildness.

4
Camping Out

After you've been day hiking a few times and are starting to get wise in the ways of the wild, you may want to try a new kind of trail experience — backpacking. Before you set off down the trail, though, be sure you've made a good start on learning the skills we talked about in the first three chapters. It's especially important to have made some "trial runs" to check out both your backpacking equipment and yourself!

Then it's time to start thinking about the nitty-gritty of staying overnight outdoors. This chapter will help you plan and prepare for your first night under the stars.

Finding a Campsite

Backpackers usually start looking for a good campsite in mid- to late afternoon — several hours before dark. It's a lot easier (and more fun) to set up camp, prepare food, clean up, and get set for the night while it's still light.

But what is a "good" campsite? Well, it's a place that won't show any traces when you leave. This kind of place can be one that has already been well used by other backpackers. There may be a fire ring with logs to sit on; tent sites may have been leveled; there may even be a pile of wood kindly left by the last campers. Another good campsite is one that hasn't been used but still won't show that you've been there. This may be a sandy, gravelly, or flat-rocked area. It could also be a dirt area with few plants and lots of bare ground.

Good campsites have several things in common. They are *found*, not made, for instance. In other words, they are places you don't need to change, except in tiny ways. For example, it's OK to move *small* rocks and twigs out of the way of your tent or sleeping bag.

Some campsites may be near water (a stream, pond, lake, creek, and so on); some may not. If the campsite your leader has planned to stay at isn't near water, members of your group will have been asked to fill their water bottles sometime during the day at a source along the way.

If there is water nearby, a good campsite is at least 300 feet from it. By camping away from the water, you'll be causing less disturbance to the wildlife that depends on it. You'll also be less likely to pollute the water. To avoid being a water polluter, always wash up (self or dishes)

well away (300 feet or more) from the stream, lake, or other water source. (There's more about dishwashing on pages 123–125.)

Finally, if you're lucky, the good site you've picked will be dry and have some flat places for sleeping. But be prepared for there to be some times when the best site available is neither flat nor dry. For example, in the northwestern part of the United States, where the weather's quite rainy, it's sometimes hard to find spots that are both dry and flat. If you're camping in the mountains, there

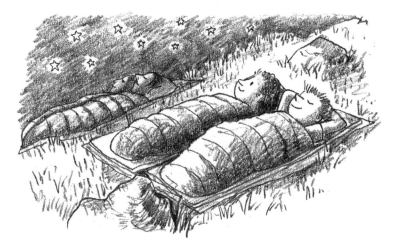

may be lots of dry spots but not many (or even not *any*) flat ones. You may have to make a choice. But this is all part of backpacking. With your friends or family and the beauties of a wild place around you, absolute flatness and dryness don't seem that important in a campsite!

Setting Up and Breaking Camp

Once you've found a good campsite, the next thing you and your group will probably do is spend some time getting your outdoor home organized. "Food first" will likely be what your stomach says as soon as a site has been chosen. But your stomach will have to wait for a few minutes before it can have what it wants. First come a few easy camp chores around your home-for-a-night.

Litter Patrol

Sometimes when you choose an already well-used campsite, it's a bit messy. Other campers may not have picked up all their litter. You may find gum wrappers, aluminum cans, toilet paper, even disposable diapers strewn around some campsites. But this doesn't mean you should pass up an otherwise good site. Instead, start your stay by taking off your packs and cleaning up the place. This takes only a few minutes and can turn a littered site into a near-ideal one. Always leave a messy site clean for the next campers rather than leaving it "as you found it."

Locating an Outdoor "Toilet"

If you're camping in a developed site — one with picnic tables and fireplaces — there'll probably be some real toilets nearby. These may be chemical toilets, pit toilets, recycling toilets, or regular flush toilets. In any case, they won't be hard to find.

But what if there aren't any "real" toilets? Well, for a quick "bush stop," just make sure you're at least 300 feet from any water source and some distance from where you'll be sleeping and eating. For solid waste "pit stops," most small groups use the "cat hole" method. Here's what you do: Again, make sure you're 300 feet or more from any water source and some distance from your campsite. Then get out your trusty trowel and dig a small hole not more than 6 inches deep (waste is broken down in the top few inches of soil). When you're finished, put

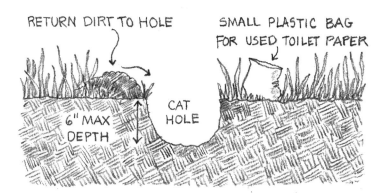

RETURN DIRT TO HOLE

SMALL PLASTIC BAG FOR USED TOILET PAPER

6" MAX DEPTH

CAT HOLE

your toilet paper in a small plastic bag (don't bury it!), fill the hole with the dirt you have just dug out, and try to make the place look like it did before.

Your leaders may suggest that part of the group use a certain area for pit stops and the rest of the group another area. This can help avoid embarrassing encounters when you have a mixed group. Also, it's a good idea for campers *not* to cluster together for this purpose. If you disperse, the area around your site won't be overused.

Large groups of backpackers or groups who are staying in one place for several days may dig a larger version of the "cat hole," called a *latrine*. If this is necessary for your group, your leaders will tell you what you need to know about it.

Setting Up

Now is the time for those in the group who are carrying part of the food for dinner to get it out. Beginners can offer to help with preparing the food. (There's more about food in the next section.) If you're not needed on the dinner crew, help locate some flat places for sleeping. If your group is using tents, help put one up. Soon you'll be able to do it alone. If the weather is good and you're sleeping on a ground cloth and foam pad, lay them out. Unroll and fluff up your sleeping bag. Get out your flashlight and put it in your pocket. Prop your pack up or lay it down nearby, where it's handy. If you have a good-sized ground cloth, the pack will probably fit on it along with your sleeping gear.

While you're in camp, try to stay inside its "boundaries." Don't walk on new territory. Keep to the paths that others have made. Of course, if the area is rocky, gravelly, sandy, or plain dirt, this is not much of a problem. Just try not to walk on plants.

Leaving the Campsite

When you're breaking camp on your last day, be sure to pick up *every* scrap of litter. (There won't be much if you've been careful.) Check the camp carefully to make sure you aren't leaving anything behind. (Did you get your toothbrush off that rock?) If the site was an untouched area to start with, it should look as if no one camped there when you leave. Put back the little rocks and twigs you moved. Sprinkle sand, dirt, leaves, or pine needles over footprints. Make everything look natural. If the site was an already-used one, it should be left spic-and-span.

Camp Cooking

On a backpacking trip, everyone gets hungry! For one thing, you've all been exercising more than usual. You've burned up a lot of fuel. Now it's breakfast, lunch, or dinner time, and you can hardly wait to eat. So what's on the menu? How soon will it be ready?

To answer the last question first, let's just say that it will be ready almost at once — if you've planned *simple* meals. Simple meals on the trail usually have three parts: (1) lots to drink; (2) a fast and easy-to-prepare main dish that includes tasty proteins and complex carbohydrates (for example, granola for breakfast, a tuna sandwich on whole wheat for lunch, and chili for dinner); (3) fruit and/or dessert.

To Heat or Not to Heat?

Nowadays, people don't cook over campfires. Instead, they use very small backpacking stoves fueled by liquid white gas, kerosene, butane, or propane. Some backpackers

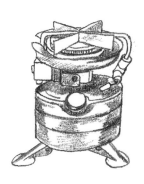

even cut their food-preparing time down by eating only "no-cook" meals. This may sound a little strange, but it makes good sense, and surprisingly good eating — especially when the weather's really warm.

Years ago, when there were only a few people camping out in wild areas, the amount of wood they used for cooking was small compared to the amount of wood available. However, because there are so many more backpackers today, using wood for cooking is no longer a good idea. If all today's backpackers cooked over wood fires, soon there would be no downed wood to decay back into the soil and help new trees and other plants grow. It wouldn't take long for our wild places to become barren and lifeless. Also, there's a great danger of starting large fires when lots of people are making campfires.

When it comes to cooking camp-out meals, beginners usually start by helping out. You may mix puddings, fetch water, stir soup, or pass out hot chocolate. Later, you'll learn how to set up and light the stove. After a few trips, you'll be ready to try a main dish, with a more experienced cook standing by ready to help. And one day you'll find yourself cooking a whole meal!

Backpacking Foods

Today's backpackers are lucky. About the only problem they have is choosing among the dozens of different kinds of

instant and freeze-dried foods available. You probably use at least a few instant foods at home now — things like instant puddings, soups, fruit drinks, mashed potatoes, ramen noodles, and macaroni and cheese. (Of course, these are only a few of the many instant foods you can find at your local supermarket and natural food store.)

Freeze-dried foods are packaged especially for hikers and backpackers. You usually find them in sporting goods and specialty backpacking stores. Some are instant, and some need a small amount of cooking. The first time you shop for freeze-dried foods, you'll have a hard time deciding what to buy. Everything sounds so good!

That's the good news. The bad news is that freeze-dried foods are rather expensive compared with other instant foods you can buy at the supermarket. Also, sad to say, although some freeze-dried foods are quite good, many don't taste as good as they sound on the labels.

On weekend backpacking trips, people often take along some fresh foods. Fruit, eggs, cheese, and even

meat are some popular choices. On longer trips, you have to carry more food, so there's less room and more weight in your pack. When you're already at your comfortable carrying limit, you won't want to take much fresh food (it's too heavy).

Each time you go backpacking, you'll learn a little more about what kinds and amounts of food suit you best. Some foods that taste good at home aren't what you want on the trail. Sometimes it's the other way around. If you take too much trail mix one time and not enough instant chocolate milk, you'll take the right amounts next time. If you were thirsty for orange juice but only had lemonade last time, you'll change that, too. If dinner took too long to cook last time, you'll bring a speedier one next time.

By now, you're probably getting the idea that you can eat pretty darned well along the trail — if you plan ahead. Here are a few tried-and-true trail-food suggestions to help you start planning.

Starting the day the granola way. If you were to walk through some weekend backpackers' campsites early in the morning, you might see the hikers guzzling water, hot chocolate, hot apple cider (instant), other fruit drinks (instant), and plain or chocolate milk (instant). After they finished their drinks, you'd probably see the hikers fixing themselves big bowls of granola (honey-toasted oats, dried fruits, nuts, and coconut) and milk (instant). In cold weather, people sometimes mix instant milk with the granola, then heat water and add it to the cereal. It's an easy way to make hot cereal. Of course, there are lots of other kinds of instant hot cereals, too. Granola gives you more energy than most others, though, because of all the nuts and fruit in it.

Then the hikers might pull out some fresh fruit. Apples, oranges, and other firm fruits last best on the trail.

This kind of cereal–instant milk–fruit breakfast takes only minutes to fix. It also doesn't leave many dirty dishes. If everybody prepares his or her own breakfast, washes his own dishes, and packs his own pack, your group will be well-fed and on the trail before you know it.

The no-dish trail lunch. If you've remembered to put your snacks and water where you can reach them, you'll probably start dipping into them soon after breakfast. Before you know it, though, it'll be time for lunch. And you'll be hungry!

At the lunch stop, maybe you'll reach into your pack for some crackers and cheese or peanut butter and jelly. Instead of crackers, some people like bagels, bread, or muffins. Other favorites are canned tuna, sardines, and sandwich spreads. If you're having lunch in camp, you'll probably want to eat this kind of easy-to-fix meal, too.

Of course, you'll drink lots of water with your lunch.

And once you've finished the main course, you can pull out the fruit (dried or fresh) and whole-grain cookies (granola bars are good, too). For this kind of meal, you don't need any dishes. Just remember to put all your trash and garbage into your litter bag. Leave nothing behind!

At lunch, you'll eat until you're not hungry, but you won't stuff yourself. If you do, going up the trail after lunch will seem like hard work, because your body will be busy digesting the food and won't have much energy left over for toting your pack.

The almost-one-pot supper. After a day of hiking, you've sweated away a lot of water. Even if you've been drinking all day, you're probably ready for more. This is why backpacking dinners almost always start out with lots of soup. There are many yummy instant soups around, and this part of the meal can be ready in minutes. All you have to do is boil some water — and add the soup, of course. (As a beginner, you won't be expected to do this. First you need to learn how to use the little backpacking stoves, but that won't take long!)

While people are slurping their soup, the cooks in your group will be putting together the main dish. Maybe it'll be a mixture of quick-cooking noodles, tuna or chicken, and cheese. Or maybe beans and cheese with tortillas on the side. Dinner could also be chili (freeze- dried, or canned if the trip is very short), spaghetti and meatballs (ditto), or rice and veggies (ditto). There are many, many ways to make a one-pot main dish. You'll probably figure out one

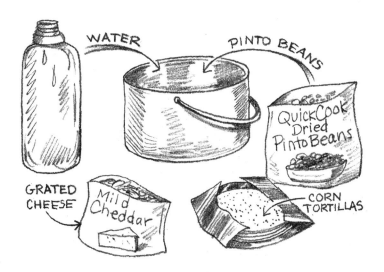

that will become your specialty. (It's a good idea to try out new ideas at home first.)

Now it's time for dessert. Everyone will have room, even though enough food may already have been put away to keep several groups of hikers going. How about some instant chocolate or butterscotch pudding? Or some instant cheesecake? Apple or blueberry cobbler (freeze-dried)? Ice cream (ditto)? Maybe a few fig bars or chocolate chip cookies? Popcorn? If you're still thirsty, how about some hot or cold apple cider or lemonade (both instant)? Well, you get the idea. In short, what you eat on the trail is limited mostly by your imagination — and, of course, by how much the food weighs!

Cleaning Up

At breakfast time, you can usually just rinse your cup and dish with water from your water bottle. At lunchtime, there usually aren't any dishes. Dinner is another story.

After dinner, there may not be many more dishes than at breakfast, but they'll probably be dirtier. So a good wash is needed. One of the easiest ways to do a good washing job quickly is to heat some water in the biggest pot. Then put part of it into a smaller, clean pot (to use for rinsing dishes). Now add just a little *biodegradable* soap to the big pot. (Biodegradable soap breaks down quickly and doesn't pollute the environment.) If the water's too hot, add enough cold water so you can just barely get your hands into it comfortably.

Have each person rinse her or his cup and/or dish before giving it to the dishwasher. Wash each piece quickly and well. Pass it to the rinser. As each piece is washed and rinsed, put it on a clean rock or log to air dry. For those times when no clean rocks or logs are nearby, some backpackers use a nylon net bag to put the clean dishes in. Then they just hang the bag up somewhere.

When you're finished washing and rinsing, pour the

"gray water" (the water you washed and rinsed the dishes in) onto a rocky or gravelly place at least 300 feet from any water source. That's all there is to it.

Any leftover food that will spoil before it can be eaten the next day needs to be put into a garbage bag. This bag should be kept tightly closed. Don't leave food out for the animals or try to feed them. Human food isn't good for wild animals. Also, having food left out for them often turns wild animals (squirrels, bears, birds, and so on) into "camp robbers."

(12 FEET ABOVE THE GROUND)

In some wild areas, all food has to be put out of the reach of camp robbers such as bears each night, as well as during the day if you are going to be away from camp. Usually food is put into a coated nylon stuff sack and/or a couple of clean, heavy-duty plastic garbage bags (one inside the other) and hauled up into a tree in a way that prevents animals from getting it down. (This works most of the time, but there are some smart bears out there who can get what they want no matter how it's put up!) Watch how experienced backpackers do this. Someday this could be one of your camp jobs.

Even if there are no bears near where you're backpacking, there may be smaller critters interested in your food. Squirrels, mice, raccoons, and even opossums have been known to carry off yummy tidbits from backpackers' camps. To discourage these little guys, put all food (and garbage) in several layers of clean, thick plastic bags so they'll have a harder time smelling it.

Also, remember *not* to keep food in your tent or on your groundcloth. Keep it either in your pack (in plastic bags) or with the rest of your group's food (in plastic bags and/or stuff sacks).

The Invisible Backpacker

It's not hard to be invisible in wild areas. At first, you have to think about it a little. You need to do some things differently than you do at home. For instance, because there aren't any trash cans, you have to carry one around with you — a litter bag.

You also need to start thinking of all wild areas as places *you* are responsible for. It wouldn't go over too well if you started walking in the flower beds, through the vegetable garden, or across the kitchen table at home or at a friend's house. And, as mentioned before, the same goes for wild places. In these places, to be responsible, backpackers use the low-impact skills we've been talking about.

Besides using low-impact skills, there are other ways a backpacker can become "invisible." For example, when your group is out in a beautiful wild area having a wonderful time, you can all try to remember that other people are there, too. One of the reasons most people backpack is to have the chance to enjoy hearing and seeing the natural world. They see enough people and hear enough city-type noise at home. They come to the forest, the seashore, the plains, the mountains, and the desert to get away from city sounds and sights. They want to enjoy the beauty and solitude undisturbed.

This doesn't mean you have to be silent or unfriendly. Talking doesn't carry far, but shouting and screaming do. It also helps if you camp as far from others as you can.

By being considerate of other campers, you're also being considerate of yourself. You'll find that you can hear the soft, smooth, feathery swoosh of an owl cruising through the trees much better if it's quiet. The sweet, fresh smells of pines or grasses or nearby water will surprise you with their richness. And the friendly sounds of the wind, the waves, and small furred and feathered creatures will surround you as you drift into sleep.

5
What's What Along the Trail

When you first start walking the trails, you may be thinking mostly about whether your pack and shoes are comfortable, how you'll get up that next hill, and when the next rest stop will be. Pretty soon, though, you won't be worrying so much about these things. You'll have broken in your pack and shoes, and you'll be in a little better shape. Now you'll start paying more attention to what you're hiking through.

Rock Talk

One of the first things you may wonder when you start looking around you more is why trails go up and down so much. Why is some land flat and some land hilly? Why are some rocks red and soft, others gray and gritty, and still others smooth and white? Why is some land full of mountains, some underwater, and some sliced with deep canyons? Geologists have been asking these questions for a long time. They've even found some answers. (*Geo* is Greek for "earth," so geologists are "earth scientists.")

But you don't have to be a geologist to read the interesting stories "written" in rocks and land. What you do need to do is look carefully around you as you hike. There are lots of clues right in front of you all the time. One interesting thing you may discover, if you look closely enough, is that rocks and sand have something in common. To see what this is, try putting together a row of rocks of different sizes. Start with one that's about the size of your little fingernail. Now find smaller and smaller rocks and line them up. After a while, the rocks will get too small for your fingers to pick up. When this happens, put a pinch of sand at the end of the row (if there's any sand around). Now you'll see why rocks and sand are alike in an important way. Sand, in fact, is made up of very tiny pieces of rock!

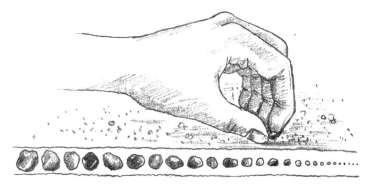

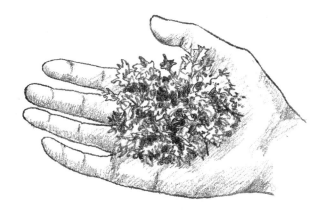

The same thing is true of dirt (or "soil," as it's sometimes called). It's just that dirt has had some things added
to the tiny pieces of rock. To see what some of these
things might be, pick up a handful of debris from under
a tree. When you sort out the debris, there'll probably be
bits of leaves from the tree, maybe some dry grass, a few
seeds, and lots of other bits and pieces of dead plants.
There'll also be some dead insects. The bits of debris will
be all different sizes, like the rocks. It's these little pieces
of dead plants and animals that get added to the little
pieces of rock to make dirt.

People don't usually think of rocks as having a "life
story," but they do. Big rocks become little rocks, which,
in turn, become sand and dirt. How do big rocks get
smaller? Well, you help — each time you step on one. But

mostly what wears rocks down are big winds, heavy rains, rivers, ocean waves, and cold and hot weather.

What builds rocks up? That is, where do rocks come from? Well, there are three main kinds of rocks — igneous, sedimentary, and metamorphic — and each is formed in a different way.

Igneous rock. The most common kind of rock is born deep in the earth, where everything is hot and liquid. (*Ignis* is a Latin word meaning "fire," so you can see where *igneous* came from.) As hot, molten, igneous material makes its long, slow way up toward the earth's cooler surface, it becomes solid. (This may take many millions of years.) When it cools off, this kind of rock is usually very hard. Granite and obsidian are igneous rocks. So is lava.

Sedimentary rock. The mud, decayed plants, and other squishy things that settle at the bottom of a pond are sediments (from the Latin word *sedimentum*, meaning "settling"). When there are many layers of sediments, the ones at the bottom get pushed and pressed together until they are hard enough to be called "rock." Sedimentary rocks aren't nearly as hard as igneous rocks. As rocks go, they are quite soft and easy to break up. Sandstone is a sedimentary rock (often reddish colored) that can have fossils in it. You can sometimes see very interesting layers of sedimentary rocks in canyons and in places where roads have been cut through hills.

Metamorphic rock. This last kind of rock was once a different kind. (*Meta* is Latin for "change," and *morphic* is from the Greek for "form." So metamorphic rock is rock that has had its form changed.) For example, under certain conditions, shale (a soft, flaky, sedimentary rock made of pressed-together mud) can be changed to slate (a hard, dark, metamorphic rock used in blackboards). This can happen when shale is under a lot of pressure, as when there are lots of layers on top of it.

By this time, you may have decided that most of what you see around you is rock in some form — and you're right. But what you see on the earth's surface is only part of the life story of rocks. The other part takes place under the earth's surface. This is where rocks are "recycled." The way this happens is that over millions and millions of years the rocks that are on the earth's surface "sink" into the earth. Some just get covered up with layers of other rocks, dirt, plants, and animals. Others are pushed under the surface of the earth when the *plates* that make up the earth's top layer bump together.

As rocks sink into the deep, hot parts of the earth, they are pushed together, melted, and changed. In a way, they become "rock stew." After a long while, the part of the "stew" that is nearest the earth's surface cools and becomes solid. Sometimes, when the plates are shoving each other around, these new, solid rocks may be pushed up as mountains or volcanoes. If the "stew" hasn't become solid yet, some may squish up through cracks in the plates and flow out of volcanoes as lava (or ooze up on the ocean floor as lava "pillows").

Did you know that this recycling of rocks and plate pushing and shoving actually move the continents

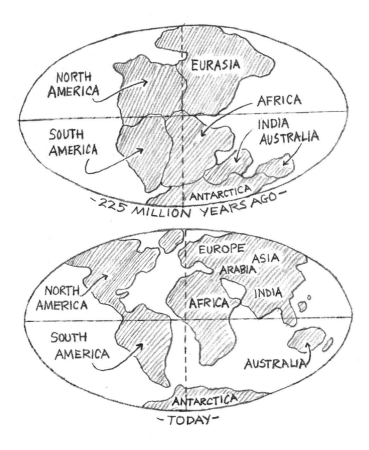

around? It's hard to believe that 225 million years ago, North America, Europe and Asia, South America, Africa, Australia, and Antarctica were all one big continent. Since then, as the plates have changed their positions, the continents have slowly gone their separate ways.

So, you see, rocks aren't just hard lumps that never change. It's just that it's hard for people to see anything but the small changes in rocks, as when a piece flakes off a cliff. Continent moving, mountain building, soil making, canyon cutting, and so on take millions of years. Sometimes — as when Mount St. Helens blew its top — dramatic changes in the landscape occur suddenly. But even though you seldom see big changes take place, you can still find out what happened by looking closely at the different kinds of rocks and lands you see around you.

Creatures Great and Small

As you hike almost any trail, all around you animals are creeping, hopping, walking, flying, burrowing, and crawling. At first you may not notice many of them, because you're busy learning basic hiking skills. Once you've gotten a grip on the basics, though, you'll begin to see and hear the creatures around you.

Some of the first animal sounds you'll notice will probably be bird songs, or maybe a woodpecker drilling holes. You may see a lizard scamper across the dusty trail or deer grazing quietly in a meadow. And they'll see and hear you. When they do, they may disappear almost instantly. But don't feel bad. As you learn ways of tuning in to the natural world, you'll see, hear, smell, and feel more and more.

You may not know that human senses aren't very sharp, compared with those of other animals. This is partly because many people live in towns, where sounds are louder. When most of the sounds you hear are loud, after a while you don't pay attention to soft sounds. In wildlands, most sounds are soft, so you have to learn to hear them.

Also, some other animals hear better than we do, some see better, some have a better sense of smell, and some can move more quickly, silently, and carefully than people can. Wild animals have developed sharp senses and fast feet to help keep them from becoming another animal's dinner. Humans have developed a big brain for the same reason.

A hawk, for instance, can see a mouse's ear flick from high in the sky. Possums and bears, however, are near-sighted. Most other animals can smell you if the wind is coming their way. If they "get wind of you," they may be off long before you get anywhere near them. Most wild animals also have a very keen sense of hearing. They may hear you and take off before you have any clue to where they *were*. People can still be good animal watchers, though, because the senses of most of our fellow creatures aren't better than those of humans in *all* these ways.

But because wild animals don't know that you only want to *watch* them, they usually make tracks away from you as soon as they know you're around. So here's where being "invisible" comes in handy again. Let's say your group has stopped for a long lunch break. You've finished eating and don't feel like napping. Instead, you quietly walk 50 paces or so away from the group to a place where you can still see them but can't hear them. Now you sit down with your back against a tree or rock, get your binoculars out, and wait.

Minutes pass. You look carefully around, trying to see every little detail: a daisylike flower in bloom, some ants carrying tiny bits of dried grass. Now a raven "craaaaks" overhead. A bluebird lands in a grassy clearing nearby, then starts darting and swooping just above the grass. What's it doing? You raise your binoculars slowly to your eyes. You find the flash of blue. It's catching little insects!

A twig cracks close by, but you keep yourself from jumping. You turn your head in the direction of the sound and see the wide, brown eyes of a deer looking you over carefully. Almost holding your breath, you look back in what you hope is a friendly way. Long seconds go by. A blink, and the deer is gone. But now there's a rustling down by your feet. A small, furry, brown mouse is scrabbling away, looking for — well, whatever mice look for. You don't know yet — seeds, maybe?

This is the way it could be. And each time you animal watch, it will be different. You'll learn to know the kinds of places where animals are likely to be. For instance, bees and some insects like flowers. Some birds like flowers, some like seeds, and some like the insects they find in trees. Mice and squirrels like seeds. Hawks and owls like mice and squirrels. And most animals have to drink some-time, whether they're deer or snakes, raccoons or rabbits, so water sources are good spots for animal watching.

You'll discover that morning and evening are the best times to see animals, especially in warm weather. (A lot of animals rest during the warmest part of the day.) You can also learn to see the signs animals leave behind: tracks, droppings, broken grass and twigs, leftover bits of peeled pine cones — and a lot more.

SOME SIGNS OF A SQUIRREL . . .

When you're watching animals, though, remember to keep your distance from them and their burrows or nests. There are several reasons this is important. One is to avoid disturbing the creatures you're watching. Another reason is that wild creatures sometimes carry diseases humans can catch. Binoculars and a small magnifying glass can help you see animals better. With binoculars, you'll be able to see some of the larger, shyer animals: elk, bighorn sheep, coyotes. Add a small magnifying glass and you'll be able to enter what is almost another world — that of nature's tiniest animals and plants.

After a few trips, your eyes, ears, and nose will have "gotten in shape" too. You'll be able to walk more quietly along the trail. You'll know where animals are likely to be spotted. You'll be seeing more and more of them, and they won't be running away from you nearly as far!

Flowers and Trees, Fruits and Seeds

Have you ever noticed that hikers talk more about seeing animals than they do about seeing plants? This is probably because animals move. Spotting them is a challenge. Plants don't move, so they're easy to spot. Or are they?

What do you see when you look at a plant? A tree, a flower, a bush — or maybe "a tall tree," "a red flower," "a small shrub." But is that all there is to plants — their size, general type, and color? Botanists (plant experts) wouldn't agree! They think that plants are as interesting as animals, but in different ways. Just because plants don't move doesn't mean they're dull. Actually, plants are very important members of our earth family. They produce oxygen and food for all of us animals, and you can't get much more important than that!

There are actually over 350,000 kinds of plants, but luckily for beginning plant watchers, there are only about six main kinds to start thinking about: flowering plants, plants with cones (*conifers*), ferns, mosses, algae, and fungi.

Flowering plants. Of the six different kinds of plants, there are more flowering plants than any others. About two-thirds of all plants are in this group. But flowering

HORSE CHESTNUT   ACORN

plants aren't just roses and dandelions. They're any plant that produces a fruit with seeds in it. And fruits aren't only peaches and apples. A coconut is a fruit. So are a walnut, an acorn, a chestnut, and a cockleburr. Grasses make fruits, as do shrubs with broad leaves, leafy vines, and trees that lose their leaves.

Conifers. These are the plants that have cones — your old friends the pine trees and their relatives. Conifers are fairly easy to pick out. Most of them have needle-like leaves (yes, those needles are *leaves*). Some, like junipers, have sort of scaly leaves. These trees and shrubs stay green all year long, so they're called "evergreens."

The seeds of conifers aren't in fruits but are hidden deep in their cones. Squirrels and woodpeckers are crazy

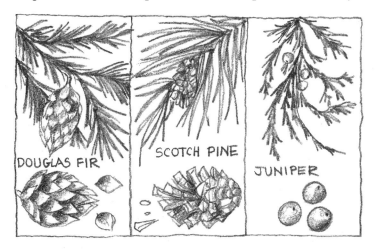

DOUGLAS FIR   SCOTCH PINE   JUNIPER

about these seeds! People like some conifer seeds, too —
especially "pine nuts," the kind found in pinyon pine
cones. (Speaking of seeds and nuts, here's a riddle for
you: Why is it that all nuts are seeds, but not all seeds are
nuts? Think about it, and maybe look up the definitions
of *nut* and *seed*.)

It's fun to try to figure out how many different kinds of
evergreens you see on a hike. You'll be surprised at how
many there are. (Young trees sometimes don't look like
mature trees. You may need a field guide to tell which is
which. See pages 158–159 for field guide suggestions.)

Ferns. This is another plant group you're probably
familiar with. It's hard to mistake the lacy fronds of a fern.

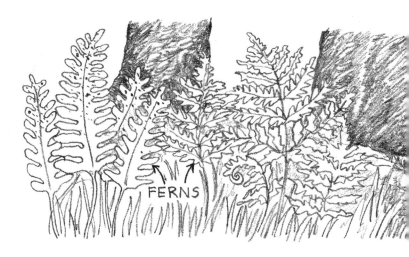

They usually grow only in forests that get quite a bit of rain, so if you hike in dry areas, you're not likely to see them. If they grow in your hiking area, see how many kinds you can find. Once more, you'll be surprised at how many there are.

Mosses. This group of plants likes damp places, too. Mosses are very small, leafy plants that reproduce by means of almost microscopic *spores* instead of seeds. (Spores have one cell; seeds have many cells.) Look for moss on rocks and tree roots at the edges of streams, ponds, rivers, and lakes. A magnifying glass is handy if you're going to look at them carefully. You'll find they have as many shapes as trees!

ALGAE (IN AN OCEAN TIDE POOL)

Algae. Did you know that the green (or red or brown) scum you see on ponds is actually a lot of little plants, and that seaweed belongs to the same group of plants? Although the plants on the pond are very tiny, they do the same things all other green plants do. They turn the energy from sunlight into simple foods and make the oxygen all animals breathe. It's the green part of a plant, the *chlorophyll*, that does the work. All green plants have it, from tall redwoods to tiny algae.

Fungi. But there's also a group of plants that isn't green. Fungi don't have chlorophyll, so they can't make food or oxygen. However, although they can't *make* food, they do *eat* food. Along with bacteria, fungi turn dead plants and animals into a kind of fertilizer that helps new

FUNGI

plants grow. Mushrooms, toadstools, and puffballs are fungi, and so is the mold that grows on bread.

Now that you've tried plant watching, you may have gotten the idea that plants are pretty interesting and important, and that really *seeing* a plant in all its complexity is a real challenge. It's especially challenging to see how each plant fits into the whole world of plants — and into the world of animals.

How It All Fits Together

After you've taken a few hikes, there are some questions you may start asking yourself. Maybe you've been watching hawks gracefully riding the rising air currents over hills and canyons, or you've come across lush, green beds of watercress at the edge of a small, clear stream. Or maybe you've been noticing the pleasant warmth of the sun on your back as you walk easily along the trail. Suddenly you start wondering why you feel so comfortable, so much a part of it all.

In fact, you start wondering why and how everything along the trail fits together. Why do you and the plants and the ants and the air and the rocks and the water and the sun and everything else seem to be all of a piece?

Why does every part, from tiniest lizard to highest mountain, seem so important?

This a large question that has a large answer. Part of the answer is that all life on earth today (including people, of course) has "grown up" over millions of years as part of a vast "family," with our world as its "house." Ecologists call this "household" an *ecosystem*. (In Greek, *eco* means "household.")

This vast ecosystem of the earth is made up of many smaller ecosystems. Some are small and relatively simple (like the ecosystem in a pond). Some are very large and complex (like a rain forest ecosystem). In each of these ecosystems, small or large, living things depend on each other — and on the land, water, and air around them. This means that when many of the trees in a forest are cut down, for instance, the forest ecosystem falls apart and the animals who once lived there lose their homes.

It's no good saying that all the animals whose habitats have been destroyed can just go live somewhere else. It doesn't work that way. *Habitats* are special kinds of places that meet the needs of certain kinds of animals. For example, people can't live and find food at the North Pole using the same kind of clothes and skills they use farther south. Monkeys from rain forests that have been destroyed can't live in an ocean or a desert. Condors can't find food in housing projects. Fringe-toed lizards can't safely hunt under the wheels of off-road vehicles.

Many plants and animals are already in deep trouble. Why? Well, when left undisturbed, all the different things that make up our world come and go. New species of plants and animals appear and others become extinct. Everything stays balanced. But when more is used up than is put back into the earth, the world's household gets unbalanced (especially if what gets put back is garbage, trash, and toxic waste). Things start to go wrong. Lakes and rivers get polluted. Tar and oil turn up in sea bird nesting sites. Too many species of plants and animals disappear.

Where You Fit In

What does all this have to do with hiking and backpacking? The answer to this question is "A lot." For one thing, when you are out there on the trail you start seeing parts of your home on earth you've never seen before (spectacular snow-capped mountains, maybe, or deep, colorful canyons). You meet some parts of your earth family you've never met (a lizard with a red, black, and white collar, perhaps — or a fluffy-tailed gray fox). You smell new scents (a certain pine's vanilla-scented bark, the sharp freshness of seaweed). Your skin even finds new worlds to explore (the fine-grained hardness of granite, the surprising silkiness of lakeshore mud).

As you become more familiar with the wilder parts of

your world, they'll start to actually feel like your "back-yard." On the trail, you'll see firsthand how some parts of our world's large and small ecosystems work. You'll see how complicated it all is. But you'll also begin to under-stand where you fit in, and you'll want to help protect this part of your earth family and your "backyard" by using the low-impact outdoor skills you've learned. You may even want to help other people protect wild places you haven't seen!

Wildlands are complicated. They have lots of parts: rocks, lizards, deer, bees, cockleburrs, pine nuts, ferns, fungi. By now you know that these all fit together pretty tightly. Plants and animals have habitats — special places where it's not too hot or too cold for them and where they can find the kinds of food they need. Plants, animals, rocks, soil, water, and air also fit together into ecosystems — groupings where everything seems to work together for the good of all. You also know that the world itself is the biggest ecosystem of all.

This is a large idea. It's almost too large to understand, except in a general way. But that's OK. As you start spending more time in wild areas, you'll understand more. Right now, you can start improving your understanding of how it all fits together in lots of small, easy ways. For example, you can work on keeping the habitats and ecosystems of our earth family together whenever you're day hiking or backpacking. How? It's easy. Leave wildlands as you find them (or in better shape). Use low-impact hiking and camping techniques. Don't take pieces of nature home with you. *Do* take photos, make sketches, and write notes. Do remember what you saw, heard, felt, and smelled (even meeting a skunk is worth remembering!). Do try to understand how it all goes together. You'll be glad you did! This book is only a start — the rest is up to you.

Books About Hiking, Nature Study, Wildlife, and More

Here are some books you can look for at your local bookstore and library. All except a few books on this list are for young people. (The adult books are noted as such.)

Geology

Silver, Donald M. *Earth, the Ever-Changing Planet*. New York, NY: Random House, 1989. Wonderfully illustrated book on the forces that have made our earth what it is today — and what it will be tomorrow. Lets you see inside a volcano, tells you how fossils got to the top of Mt. Everest, clues you in on why the continents are always on the move, and lots more. (For more on geology, see "Nature Study," on pages 158–159.)

Hiking and Backpacking

Boy Scouts of America. *Field Book*. Irving, TX: Boy Scouts of America, 1984. Interesting guide to just about every wild-area activity you can think of.

Fletcher, Colin. *The Complete Walker III*. New York, NY: Alfred A. Knopf, 1984. A very complete what-to-take and how-to-do-it book for all hikers. Sometimes called "the walker's Bible." (Adult)

Freeman, Tony. *Beginning Backpacking*. Chicago, IL: Children's Press, 1980. A short book, but with good photographs and good advice.

Thomas, Art. *Backpacking Is for Me*. Minneapolis, MN: Lerner Publications, 1980. Another short book with good photos and good advice.

Nature Study

Audubon Society Beginner's Guides. New York, NY: Random House. These small, well-illustrated books are just the thing for the beginning naturalist. Look for titles such as *Birds, Rocks & Minerals, Wildflowers*, and *Reptiles & Amphibians*.

Brown, Vinson. *Investigating Nature Through Outdoor Projects*. Harrisburg, PA: Stackpole Books, 1983. This book will help you uncover the secrets of the wildlife community in your backyard and garden, and in woods, ponds, and streams. Learn to read the behavior of all kinds of extraordinary creatures, from squirrels to birds to doodlebugs to spiders. Also look for *The Secret Languages of Animals* and *Reading the Outdoors by Night*, by the same author.

Discovering Science Series. New York, NY: Facts on File Publications. Some titles to look for in this nicely illustrated series are *Looking at Animals, How Animals Behave*, and *Air, Water, & Weather*.

Endangered Earth Series. New York, NY: Crown Publishers. Some plants and animals are having a hard time surviving on earth today. This very well illustrated series will tell you about several ways people can help them. Some titles to look for are *Environment, Land Animals*, and *Birds*.

Eyewitness Books. New York, NY: Alfred A. Knopf. There are several books in this excellent series. Look for titles such as *Plant, Rocks*

& Minerals, Tree, Butterfly & Moth, Mammal, and Bird. Hundreds of spectacular photos make each one seem like your own private, living mini-wilderness and museum.

Golden Guides Series. New York, NY: Golden Press. You can hold these guides in the palm of your hand, so they're very "handy." Some of the many titles to look for are Mammals, Stars, and Weather.

Library of Knowledge Series. New York, NY: Random House. There are several titles in this well-done series. Look for The Animal World, Astronomy Today, and Life on Earth. All are full of wonderfully interesting illustrations.

Penny, Malcolm. The Food Chain. New York, NY: The Bookwright Press, 1988. Find out all about the eaters and the eaten in this interestingly illustrated book on how animals fit into the chain of life.

Photography

Owens-Knudsen, Vick. Photography Basics: An Introduction for Young People. New York, NY: Prentice-Hall, 1983. This book takes you right inside a camera, as well as into a darkroom where you'll see just what it takes to develop photos. You'll also learn how to take a good picture and how to produce special effects.

Van Wormer, Joe. How to Be a Wildlife Photographer. New York, NY: Lodestar Books, 1982. Learn about backgrounds, viewpoints, lights, cameras, and action — everything you need to know to take good animal pictures.

Places to Go

Foster, Lynne, Exploring the Grand Canyon — Adventures of Yesterday & Today. Grand Canyon, AZ: Grand Canyon Natural History Association, 1990. Find out how the Grand Canyon became grand, ride the rapids with Colorado River runners, discover canyon plants and animals, and learn where to hike when you visit this spectacular national park.

Rand McNally Campground & Trailer Park Guide — West/East. Skokie, IL: Rand McNally Campground Publications, 1989. Includes sites in state parks and forests, national parks and forests, Bureau of Land Management areas, backpack access areas, private facilities, and others. Facilities and prices included. Published yearly. (Adult)

Sierra Club Guides to the National Parks Series. San Francisco, CA: Sierra Club Books. Brief descriptions of wild areas good for hiking and backpacking. Titles include the following areas: *Desert Southwest, East and Middle West, Pacific Northwest and Alaska, Pacific Southwest and Hawaii,* and *Rocky Mountains and the Great Plains.* (Adult)

Young, Donald, with Cynthia Overbeck Bix. *The Sierra Club Book of Our National Parks.* San Francisco, CA: Sierra Club Books/Little, Brown, 1990. This book explores the past, present, and future of our national park system.

Star Gazing

Thompson, C. E. *Constellations — A Field Guide for Young Stargazers.* New York, NY: Grosset & Dunlap, 1989. The illustrations in this book glow in the dark, so you can use it outside at night! Learn what the major constellations look like at different seasons of the year and read the legends telling how they got their names.

Survival How-to

Brown, Tom, Jr. *Tom Brown's Field Guide to Nature & Survival for Children.* New York, NY: Berkley Books, 1989. Contains information on how to survive in the wilderness under just about any conditions.

Trail Food and Cooking

Axcell, Claudia, Diane Cooke, and Vikki Kinmont. *Simple Foods for the Pack*. San Francisco, CA: Sierra Club Books, 1986. Good and easy trail eats. (Adult)

Wayfinding

McVey, Vicki, *The Sierra Club Wayfinding Book*. San Francisco, CA: Sierra Club Books/Little, Brown, 1989. This fascinating book will take you on an exciting trip through the history of wayfinding and show you how to find your own way to (and from) just about anywhere.

Weather

Lambert, David, and Ralph Hardy. *Weather & Its Work*. New York, NY: Facts on File, 1985. Get the inside information on what causes thunder, lightning, tornadoes, hurricanes, and just plain old everyday weather. Great photos and illustrations.

Pettigrew, Mark. *Weather*. New York, NY: Gloucester Press, 1987. Clear illustrations and photos help take the mystery out of weather. Includes instructions for making your own simple weather station.

Wildlife

(See also the various series mentioned in "Nature Study," above.)

Animal Kingdom Series. New York, NY: Bookwright Press. Some titles to look for in this wonderfully illustrated series are *Animal Camouflage, Animal Evolution, Animal Homes, Animal Migration,* and *Animals & Their Young*.

Arnosky, Jim. *Secrets of a Wildlife Watcher*. New York, NY: Lothrop, Lee & Shepard, 1983. Get in on the secrets of using binoculars, finding animals, and getting close enough to watch them. Lots of wildlife-watching tips for beginners and old hands alike.

Fadala, Sam. *Basic Projects in Wildlife Watching*. Harrisburg, PA: Stackpole Books, 1989. The projects described in this book are so exciting that once you get your hands on it, you'll immediately want to rush right out the door and get started sharpening your senses, making yourself invisible, decoding earth messages, and much more.

Parker, Steve. *Be an Animal Detective*. New York, NY: Derrydale Books/Crown Publishers, 1989. While you're enjoying the great illustrations in this book, you'll also be finding out how animal families behave, why some animals are in danger, what a "food web" is, and lots more.

Peterson's First Guides Series. Boston, MA: Houghton Mifflin. If you're interested in learning how to identify furry and feathered critters (as well as wildflowers and even stars in the sky), try these palm-sized, colorfully illustrated guides. Titles include *Birds, Mammals, Wildflowers,* and *Astronomy*.

What to Take and Where to Get It

The first two lists here contain the "musts," the "very useful," and the "for fun" pieces of equipment for day hiking and backpacking that were described and explained in Chapter 1. Next is a list of tried-and-true trail foods. And the last list will help you start your own collection of hiking and backpacking equipment.

Day-Hiking Start-up Gear List

Musts

Day pack (small)
Water bottle(s) (1 qt. or 1 l. size, wide mouth)
Water
Athletic shoes (sturdy, well broken in)
Socks (part cotton, thick)
Food (see below for suggestions)
Hat (with brim for warm weather, or covering ears for cool weather)
Extra clothes (light- or medium-weight jacket, depending on the
    weather; windbreaker; gloves or mittens for cool weather)
Plastic or metal whistle
Sunglasses
Sunblock (lotion and lip balm)
Small flashlight with extra batteries and bulb

Musts (continued)

Map and/or trail guide
Watch
"Mini" first aid kit
Coins for phone calls

Very Useful

Small paper or plastic bag
Bandanna(s)
Large plastic garbage bag
Toilet paper
Notebook and pencil or pen

For Fun

Binoculars
Camera
Magnifying glass (small)

Backpacking Start-up Gear List

Musts

Everything on the "Day-hiking Start-up Gear List"
Backpack
Trail boots or shoes (well broken in)
Sleeping bag (3 lbs. or under, with synthetic fill), waterproof stuff
  sack, and nylon straps for attaching sleeping bag to backpack
Sleeping pad (⅜-inch, closed cell) or thin, self-inflating air
  mattress, and waterproof stuff sack
Ground cover (tube tent or waterproof tarp at least 3 ft. by 7½ ft.)
Cup
Spoon
Deep dish
Toothbrush (small)

Comb/brush (small)
Towel and washcloth (small and thin)
Clothes (select from the list below according to the season
   and weather):
      socks (light inner, part-wool outer)
      long-sleeved shirt
      short-sleeved shirt
      wool shirt or sweater
      long pants
      shorts
      jacket (medium weight, synthetic fill, with hood)
      underclothes
      windbreaker (with hood)
      watch cap or balaclava
      gloves or mittens
      Food (see below for suggestions)

Very Useful

Tent (this comes later for you, but some people in your group
   may have them)
Rain gear (poncho or rain jacket with hood)
Small plastic trowel (marked in inches or centimeters)
30 feet of light (⅛-inch) nylon cord
Safety pins
Biodegradable soap (for self and dishes)
Insect repellent
Identification
Plastic bags and ties (small to large; to put your clothes, food,
   and so on in to keep them organized)

For Fun

Books (field books, guidebooks, other)
Games ("travel" size)
Day pack (for side trips)
Swimsuit

Items Leaders Will Bring

Water purification tablets and/or water filter
First aid kit ("maxi")
Waterproofed matches
Compass
Backpacking stove and fuel
Cooking equipment
Pocket knife
Insect repellent
Repair kit

Trail Food Suggestions

You'll probably be bringing your own snacks, and maybe your own breakfasts and lunches. The more experienced backpackers in your group probably will be bringing food for dinners. This list of suggestions is for breakfasts, lunches, and snacks only.

Whole-grain breads (English muffins, regular muffins, tortillas, crackers, pocket bread, sweet breads, etc.)
Whole-grain cereals (honey-sweetened granola with lots of dried fruits and nuts, instant oatmeal, raisin bran, etc.)
Instant dried milk
Instant hot chocolate, apple cider, etc.
Instant fruit juices (freeze-dried crystals — remember to use two to three times more water than directions call for)
Trail mix (with lots of dried fruit, nuts, seeds, coconut, etc.)
Fruit (fresh, fruit "chips," fruit "leather," dried or dehydrated)
Whole-grain cookies and snack ("granola") bars
Nonmeltable candy (high-energy bars made with fruit, nuts, honey, etc.; sesame seed candy like halvah or seed bars with honey; hard candy)
Cheese ("string" cheese doesn't seem to melt easily, and there are even "squeeze" cheeses)
Nut butters (peanut, almond, sunflower, etc.)

Jams and jellies sweetened with honey or fruit juice
Hard-boiled eggs
Sardines (small, easy-open cans)
Tuna (packed in water, small, easy-open cans)
Lunchmeat spreads (in small, easy-open cans)

Places to Write for Gear Catalogs

These are just a few of the companies that sell hiking and backpacking gear (including foods) by mail. Most of their catalogs are free. Once you get on the mailing list of one of these companies by asking for a catalog, other companies selling this kind of gear may also send you catalogs without your asking for them! Some companies have retail stores all over the United States.

Campmor, Inc.
810 Route #17N
Paramus, New Jersey 07652

Don Gleason's Campers Supply, Inc.
P. O. Box 87
Northampton, Massachusetts 01061-0087

Eddie Bauer, Inc.
15010 NE 36th Street
Redmond, Washington 98052

L. L. Bean, Inc.
Casco Street
Freeport, Maine 04033

Recreational Equipment, Inc. (REI)
P. O. Box 88125
Seattle, Washington 98138-0125

Where to Write for Trail Information

The list below may look short, but it actually covers a lot of ground. Each agency (or department) manages many square miles of public lands.

Information on Public Lands Managed by City, State, and U.S. Government Departments

The people in city, county, and state government departments can give you lots of information about hiking in your local, regional, and state parks. They'll often send you free brochures and maps. For their phone numbers and addresses, look in your telephone book under the city, county, and state government listings. Also try looking under the "U.S. Government" listings for local offices of departments listed below.

Bureau of Land Management (BLM)
Office of Information
Department of the Interior
Washington, D.C. 20240
(You may be surprised at how much of the public land near where you live is managed by this agency. The BLM doesn't put up many signs!)

National Park Service (NPS)
Department of the Interior
Washington, D.C. 20240
(The NPS also manages the National Trail System. This system includes National Historic Trails, National Recreation Trails, and National Scenic Trails.)

U.S. Fish & Wildlife Service (FWS)
Department of the Interior
Washington, D.C. 20240

U.S. Forest Service (USFS)
Department of Agriculture
Box 2417
Washington, D.C. 20013

Information on Canadian Public Lands

The Canadian government departments that manage public lands are happy to provide hiking information. The department that manages most of Canada's public lands is called Parks Canada. Below are the addresses of the major Parks Canada offices.

Parks Canada, Atlantic Region
Upper Water Street
Halifax, Nova Scotia B3J 1S9
Canada

Parks Canada, Quebec Region
Post Office Box 2474
Postal Terminal
Quebec G1K 7R3
Canada

Parks Canada, Ontario Region
111 East Water Street, Box 1359
Cornwall, Ontario K6H 6S3
Canada

Parks Canada, Prairie Region
Confederation Building, 457 Main Street
Winnipeg, Manitoba R3B 1B4
Canada

Parks Canada, Western Region
5th Floor, 220 4th Avenue S.E./Box 2989, Station M
Calgary, Alberta T2P 3H8
Canada

Information on Topographic Maps

Remember to write for the state index first (these are free). In addition to the index you ask for, the USGS will send you ordering and price information.

U.S. Geological Survey (USGS)
Branch of Distribution
1200 S. Eads Street
Arlington, Virginia 22202
(For maps east of the Mississippi River)

USGS
Branch of Distribution
Box 25286
Federal Center
Denver, Colorado 80225
(For maps west of the Mississippi River)

Department of Energy, Mines, & Resources
615 Booth Street
Ottawa, Ontario K1A 0E4
Canada
(For maps covering Canadian provinces)

Some Groups That Sponsor Hikes

The organizations listed below have chapters all over the United States and/or Canada. To get in touch with them, first look in your local telephone book. If an organization isn't listed in the telephone book, write to the address below for information on the chapter nearest to you.

Also look in your telephone book for the numbers and addresses of the recreation and/or parks departments that may be listed under the name of your city and/or county. These departments often sponsor hiking activities.

American Hiking Society
1015-31st Street, NW
Washington, D.C. 20007

Appalachian Mountain Club
5 Joy Street
Boston, Massachusetts 02108

Audubon Society
950 Third Avenue
New York, New York 10022

Boy Scouts of America
1325 Walnut Hill Lane
Irving, Texas 75038

Boy Scouts of Canada
National Council Offices
P. O. Box 5151, Station F
Ottawa, Ontario K2C 3G7
Canada

Boys and Girls Clubs of Canada
National Office
250 Consumers Road, #505
Willowdale, Ontario M2J 4V6
Canada

Campfire Girls of America
4608 Madison Avenue
Kansas City, Missouri 64112

Federation of Western Outdoor Clubs
431 Green Glen Way
Mill Valley, California 94941

Girl Guides of Canada
50 Merton Street
Toronto, Ontario M4S 1A3
Canada

Girl Scouts of America
830 Third Avenue & 51st Street
New York, New York 10022

The Mountaineers
300 Third Avenue W
Seattle, Washington 98119

National Wildlife Federation
1412-16th Street NW
Washington, D.C. 20036

The Nature Conservancy
1800 N. Kent Street, Suite 800
Arlington, Virginia 22209

Sierra Club
730 Polk Street
San Francisco, California 94109

Young Men's Christian Association (YMCA)
101 N. Wacker Drive
Chicago, Illinois 60606

Young Women's Christian Association (YWCA)
726 Broadway
New York, New York 10003

YMCA Canada
160 Yonge Street
Toronto, Ontario M4S 2A9
Canada

YWCA Canada
80 Gerrard Street East
Toronto, Ontario M5B 1G6
Canada

Index